MW01071492

PRE-MARITAL COUNSELING

A guide for therapists and counselors, *Pre-Marital Counseling* addresses the common problems couples face when starting or considering marriage. This step-by-step guide teaches specific intervention strategies for common pre-marital problems, such as financial stress, blending families, and mental health issues. It also teaches readers helpful skills such as developing empathy, learning to compromise, and communicating successfully, all within a potentially diverse client population. Skurtu further helps clinicians personalize their assessment and treatment plans for each couple so that they have realistic expectations. Written by a certified sex therapist, there is also a unique chapter on helpful sex education tips for maintaining desire in long-term relationships.

Angela Skurtu, MEd, LMFT, is a certified sex therapist and licensed marriage and family therapist in Ballwin, Missouri.

"*Pre-Marital Counseling* is a wonderfully engaging book for clinicians interested in helping couples to build strong and lasting relationships. Through a vivid array of stories, exercises, and interventions, Angela Skurtu provides a framework to promote healthy habits of successful relationships. Whether as a session-by-session guide or an in-the-moment resource, this book has something for both new and seasoned therapists!"—**Bob Bertolino, PhD**, is professor of rehabilitation counseling at Maryville University and author of *The Therapist's Notebook for Families*.

"If you have ever wanted all the helpful pre-commitment clinical recommendations for couples in one place, this is your book! This insightful book offers clinicians a very accessible, clear, and helpful guide in working with couples who are seeking a more intimate commitment with one another. Angela shares her knowledge and ideas in a way that enables any practitioner to support couples in knowing each other better and loving each other longer."—**Tiffany B. Brown, PhD, LMFT**, holds a doctoral degree in marriage and family therapy, and is currently teaching in the Couples and Family Therapy Program at the University of Oregon.

"Consciously speaking about the challenging issues of marriage as much as possible before saying 'I do' is a great start for any couple. Angela Skurtu communicates clearly and lively about all the traditional pre-marital counseling topics (values, money, children, etc.), but her added gift is presenting a thoughtful outline for addressing sexual concerns/expectations in a very sex-positive manner."—**Brian Cross, PhD**, is a certified sex therapist in private practice in Washington, D.C.

"Clinicians working with couples know that the best time to give them a chance at marital success is before negative patterns are ingrained. But couples in love don't want to admit to problems. They may, however, consider taking a pre-marital counseling course. That's where Angela Skurtu's *Premarital Counseling: A Guide for Clinicians* can be useful for clinicians. In short, readable, topical chapters Skurtu outlines a six- to eight-week course that addresses common relationship problems.

Skurtu's short book should be invaluable for young clinicians, but also offers a useful framework for experienced counselors who want to add premarital counseling to their list of offerings."—**Ronald Scott, PhD**, is a psychologist and is currently the training program coordinator for Care and Counseling in St. Louis, Missouri.

"This book provides easy to follow instructions for helping premarital couples. Hitting on all the important topics that clinicians need to be aware of when counseling couples, Angela does an excellent job of combining clinical techniques and the latest research to provide a comprehensive guidebook. I would recommend this book for any clinicians who are seeking to strengthen their existing skills or are beginning work in this area."—**Brian James Willoughby, PhD**, is an assistant professor in the School of Family Life at Brigham Young University

PRE-MARITAL COUNSELING

A Guide for Clinicians

Angela Skurtu, MEd, LMFT

Routledge
Taylor & Francis Group

NEW YORK AND LONDON

First published 2016
by Routledge
711 Third Avenue, New York, NY 10017

and by Routledge
2 Park Square, Milton Park, Abingdon, Oxon, OX14 4RN

Routledge is an imprint of the Taylor & Francis Group, an informa business

Library of Congress Cataloging in Publication Data
A catalog record for this book has been requested

ISBN: 978-1-138-82876-6 (hbk)
ISBN: 978-1-138-82877-3 (pbk)
ISBN: 978-1-315-73809-3 (ebk)

Typeset in Baskerville
by Florence Production Ltd, Stoodleigh, Devon, UK

Printed and bound in the United States of America by Publishers Graphics,
LLC on sustainably sourced paper.

CONTENTS

PREFACE

There once was an Orthodox Jewish couple who had been married for over 40 years. Every week, they sat down at a table across from each other and apologized. They apologized for not saying thank you last Saturday. They apologized for staying late at work on Monday. They apologized for leaving their underwear on the floor every morning. This habit offered opportunities for them to practice being humble and apologetic and often helped each of them individually feel more appreciated. The most successful relationships are a system of habits like this one. This book teaches clinicians how to provide pre-marital counseling based on five healthy habits for successful relationships.

There are a handful of professionally published, peer-reviewed books in the area of pre-marital counseling. Of the books available, the typical audience is the couples planning to marry. This book is written primarily for mental health clinicians. Couples interested in this topic can also follow along.

This book contains a framework for creating pre-marital treatment plans for engaged couples or couples considering marriage, based on an 8-week program. The program includes assessment and treatment planning, five healthy habits for successful relationships, individualized problem-solving suggestions, and termination.

I am a Licensed Marriage and Family Therapist in the state of Missouri and a Certified Sex Therapist through the American Association of Sex, Educators, Counselors, and Therapists. I received my Masters of Education in Couples, Family and Human Services, and have been offering marriage counseling for over six years. I also run a private practice built upon the principles covered in this book.

The information in this book comes from my own education and research, including the stories told by both clients and couples in my life who are in successful marriages. The information also comes from the very struggles I have overcome in my own marriage.

I use the habits discussed in this book daily to teach couples how to create lasting marriages. The habits help struggling couples rebuild their relationships and help newly formed couples create the foundation for a healthy relationship.

As counselor, you'll play a valuable role in the lives of your clients. People consider mental health clinicians experts about marriage. Part of becoming an expert is not only learning the most applicable skills available to clients, but also putting those skills into practice. I encourage you to practice the skills you learn in this book in your personal relationships until they become habits of your own. Not only will this make you a pro, but it will also give you valuable life lessons and insights that can be used as an example for clients struggling to develop the same habits.

To get you started, complete the following exercises:

1. Do some personal research about marriage and create your own definition for what a healthy marriage looks like.
2. Interview two or more couples who are happily married. Find out their advice for what it took to make their relationship succeed.
3. Clearly identify your values regarding relationships. How might your values alter the way you work with a client who has a very different belief system?

After you have completed the above tasks, use your answers as a reference point going forward in this book. As you read each chapter, evaluate how your personal values and understandings about marriage are similar or different to the topics discussed.

I encourage you to keep an open mind and a willingness to learn. The ultimate goal of this book is to help clinicians teach couples valuable skills for positive relationships. Couples who consistently practice those skills develop habits that lead to successful marriages.

When you are finished reading this book, you will be able to provide competent pre-marital counseling based on these habits. Marriage is a system of habits: given practice, couples can achieve a healthy, satisfying relationship long term.

ACKNOWLEDGEMENTS

I have plenty of people to thank for the creation of this book. First, Kristen Reed Edens, a local editor, helped me create the proposal and gave me the courage to believe I could write a book. Second, my intern, Amy Holt, helped me find recent research on various topics included in the book. My husband, Joshua Skurtu, helped periodically by offering support, reminding me to stay on task, and occasionally helping with editing. I would also like to thank Bob Bertolino for answering a multitude of questions throughout the writing and editing process. Finally, my reviewers Miriam DeBerry, Denise LaBarge, and Amy Treadwell gave me feedback for how to add helpful content for the book. Thank you all for the support and guidance.

INTRODUCTION

We were perfectly happy until we decided to live happily ever after.
Sarah Jessica Parker, *Sex and the City*

Looking back at your own marriage, what would you have liked to have known before you got married? What are the important questions couples need to answer? How can we, as clinicians, be confident that we have set our clients on the best possible path to a healthy marriage? The goal of pre-marital counseling and this book is to answer these questions.

Some couples who divorce answer that they should have known better. "From the beginning, he was a jerk," they might say or "next time, I will pick someone who doesn't have anger issues." While picking a good mate is still an important piece to a healthy marriage, many married couples have learned that being a good person alone doesn't necessarily lead to happy marriages. The choices one makes or the habits developed in the relationship also lead to the success of the relationship. People who report having happy marriages typically have learned certain habits that contribute to those successful relationships.

Couples who have long-lasting marriages do things differently. I refer to these couples as the experts on marriage because true marriage experts are the couples who have made it through the good, the bad, and the ugly and still love each other as much, if not more, than the day they first married. What these marriage experts know is that marriage requires work to survive. Clinicians play a vital role by teaching couples the habits that can lead to happy marriages.

What is the real difference between couples who make it work and couples who struggle? Let's start by saying that marriage is hard and every couple will struggle at some point in their relationship. There is a reason we study marriage: it's a complex system that involves two people working together to accomplish individual goals, mutual couple goals, and family goals. However, there are some couples who struggle through their lives a little better than others. There are couples who go through struggles and find themselves growing apart. At the same time, other couples go through these struggles feeling closer and stronger. Those couples who develop healthy habits tend to fair better overall.

As clinicians, we are in a complex position to guide couples. In pre-marital counseling, couples rely on us to provide the tools to make their marriages work. The information provided in this book discusses researched tools and habits that the experts of marriage already have learned on their own. I encourage you to use this book as your guide in leading pre-marital couples to their own success stories.

History of Pre-Marital Advice

Prior to the mid-1800s, people did not marry for love. Most couples married for political, social, or economic gain (Coontz, 2005). A couple's family played a crucial role in deciding whom their children would marry (Campbell and Wright, 2010). Individuals widely accepted that marriages for love were not a smart move, as passion tended to die over time.

> *A passionate love cannot by the very nature of our emotional faculties be retained at full tension always, and what it is to happen, when for the moment the harp must be unstrung? Unless there is a less taut tie of mutual respect and common interests, it is like enough that the harp will not be restrung at all. Disillusioned, disgusted, chilled to the soul, you will leave the fine instrument under the cover in the corner of your drawing-room, and seek for other music to fill the empty house.*
>
> Robert F. Horton, "On the Art of
> Living Together," 1896

Since the family was primarily responsible for picking a mate, they would likely be more interested in a partner who could provide stability for their daughter than one who fulfills her heart's desires.

After the Industrial Revolution, or the mid-1800s, marriage began shifting toward love and personal fulfillment (Campbell and Wright, 2010). At this time, people started to offer more pre-marital advice. The oldest pre-marital advice recorded can be found in the early 1800s. The advice of the time typically focused on teaching individuals how to pick a good mate. To pick a good mate, couples were advised to consider a variety of factors.

In the first place, see the girl you intend to honor as early in the morning as possible, and note whether she is fresh and tidy or limp and frowsy.
   Watch how she treats her pets-her dog, her canary, her little sisters . . .
   Remember if she makes a habit of walking or driving.
Anon. approximately 1900 (quoted in
Beachcombing, 2011)

Picking a good mate helped a man or a woman ensure their relationship would be healthy. It was important to choose a good mate during this time because an individual would likely spend their entire life with this person. Divorce was not as accepted or common. An individual needed to pick well or they would lead a very unhappy life.

After WWII, the divorce rates in the US rose drastically. At this time, several marriage experts stepped in to help give couples advice. Initially these "experts" were not necessarily trained in marriage therapy or psychology. They were popular advice-givers interested in the topic who believed that marriages could be saved and divorce prevented (Celello, 2009; Tartakovsky, 2012). After some time, the first formal Marriage and Family Therapists appeared with the founding of the American Association of Marriage Counselors in 1942. The marriage counselors typically offered suggestions for choosing a mate and suggested behaviors to ensure the stability of the marriage.

The marriage advice offered today varies greatly from how to keep the spark in your marriage to how to split the chores. The advice typically discusses behaviors couples can do to keep their relationship working well. A brief web search reveals the advice is coming from psychologists, recently divorced people, pastors, and more. Through the internet, couples have instant access to a variety of tools and resources.

As a society, Americans continue to research and learn about the qualities necessary to maintain a healthy marriage. Some of the qualities that have continued to be helpful across time will be found in this book. Other suggestions offered will be new advice based on the most recent research. However, research by its very nature is always changing and evolving. To provide the best treatment, clinicians must continue to evolve and grow with the expanding research of our time. When you use this book, keep the pieces that continue to be helpful and add the pieces that you learn in your own practice.

Role of the Therapist in Pre-Marital Counseling

In the 1998 movie *A Night at the Roxbury*, Will Farrell and Molly Shannon stand before their friends and family taking their wedding vows. When Will Farrell is asked, "Do you take this woman to be your lawfully wedded wife . . ." he responds, "My dad already paid the caterer." Whether we like it not, our clients don't always have the best reason for why they are getting married. However, it is not our job to convince couples to avoid marriage. It is our job to provide clients with the best possible outcomes in marriage, regardless of whether or not they are a good match in our eyes.

Historically, therapists and pastors have seen their role in pre-marital counseling as a gatekeeper to marriage. Clinicians typically try to educate couples on the realities of marriage and to give honest advice about whether they see this marriage succeeding, given what they have learned about the couple. The problem with this role is that usually couples are going to get married whether or not you approve. Ask any couple who was "warned" about their upcoming marriage whether that warning led them to change their plans. Most likely it doesn't change plans. The caterer has been paid! The dress purchased! The honeymoon planned! This couple is getting married!

Rather than putting yourself in the position of gatekeeper, I advocate you to take the role of educator and guide. Your couples come to you for answers on how to make their marriage work. They love each other, they have already made a commitment to marriage, and now they are taking an important step of preparing to do marriage well. This step already puts them at an advantage to their peers since approximately 19 percent of couples today actually seek any type of marital counseling (Parker-Pope, 2010).

Your role is to give your couples the most clear and accurate view of what marriage looks like and how to have a healthy, stable marriage. Unless there is a clear situation of danger to self or others (i.e. intimate partner violence (IPV), untreated mental illness, or something that is currently damaging to either partner such as secret affairs), it really is not your position to tell a couple whether or not they should marry.

When you look at couple relationships that have lasted 20 years, 30 years, and full lifetimes, they don't all start out perfectly and they don't all look the same. One of the themes of John Gottman's (1995) book *Why Marriages Succeed or Fail* taught clinicians that couples of all kinds have successful marriages. Focus your attention on learning the best possible habits to teach couples. From this knowledge, trust couples to make the best decisions for themselves about their upcoming marriage or long-term relationship.

Benefits of Pre-Marital Counseling

There are several benefits couples will gain in pre-marital counseling. Couples who participate in marriage preparation are 79 percent better off than non-participants (Carroll and Doherty, 2003) in the areas of "enhanced communication and conflict management skills, more commitment to one's mate, greater positivity in marriage, and reduced chances for divorce" (Duncan, Childs, and Larson, 2010, p. 623). In our clinical work, we have access to a wide variety of tools to teach couples how to better communicate, resolve conflict and increase relationship satisfaction. In this book, I will cover several skills that have helped the couples in my practice, but I also encourage you to include skills your clients have benefitted from as well.

In addition to specific skills, this book will also teach clinicians how to tailor their treatment to address specific problems each individual couple may face. The current research suggests that therapists who tailor their treatment more specifically to each couple have better outcomes (Duncan, Childs, and Larson, 2010). While most pre-marital counseling programs typically teach couples better communication and problem-solving skills, further emphasis should focus on the specific needs of the couple (Fawcitt et al., 2010). These issues could include differences in religious or moral values, lack of financial planning, or inability to set clear boundaries with in-laws or outsiders. In Chapter 7, clinicians will learn how to modify their pre-marital treatment to address these specific concerns.

Finally, you as a clinician will also benefit from offering pre-marital counseling. Couples who choose pre-marital counseling have lower divorce rates and higher levels of marital quality (Fawcitt et al., 2010). It is rewarding to know that your work with a couple is potentially preventing a divorce. In addition, you will typically find this group of clients to be highly motivated to learn and more open to make changes in their relationship. Part of the reason for this is that couples in the beginning of their relationship tend to have more patience for one another. This makes it very easy to offer suggestions for change.

Myths about Pre-Marital Counseling

Pre-marital education has become more popular in recent times. Pre-marital education can be traced back to the 1930s, when the earliest pre-marital counseling was offered by churches (Duncan, Childs, and Larson, 2010). While more couples show interest in getting help before problems start, many of the couples are not interested in seeking religious education programs. Due to this change, more couples are seeking pre-marital counseling from clinicians.

Another reason for more interest in pre-marital counseling may be a result of adult children who came from divorced backgrounds. Increasing numbers of adults are first and second generations of children whose parents divorced. They have seen the repercussions of divorce in their lives and the lives of their friends and family. Couples are seeking advice from experts and want to learn the tools necessary to keep their marriages healthy.

Due to this recent shift, there are several myths about pre-marital counseling and what type of help is available. These myths include ideas about who should receive pre-marital counseling, and what it is used for. In order to dispel a few of these myths, I will describe a few that I commonly encounter in my own practice.

Myth #1: Pre-marital counseling is meant primarily for couples between the ages of 19–29.

Reality: Couples of any age can benefit from pre-marital counseling. The skills discussed in this book focus on healthy collaborative habits. People who master these habits will find that they experience gains in a variety of relationships including their partnerships, sibling relationships, and parent/child relationships. Counseling is a lifetime skill that is beneficial toward all relationships.

Myth #2: Pre-marital counseling is only meant for couples who have never been married.

Reality: Divorced individuals sometimes make the same mistakes in newer relationships. We have all heard the stories of people who marry, remarry, and remarry again. One of the biggest challenges an individual must overcome after a divorce is to look past the blaming of their partner to the areas they personally could have worked on to make things better. In every marriage there are two people who contribute to the health or the demise of a marriage. Previously divorced partners can benefit from pre-marital counseling by learning pro-social skills, learning how to effectively navigate co-parenting with a new partner, and by making a plan of action for potential problems going forward.

Myth #3: Pre-marital counseling is primarily meant for couples who plan to get married.

Reality: Couples who cohabit or choose not to marry can still benefit from pre-marital counseling. Research shows that couples who cohabit or have not been paired yet may benefit more from receiving pre-marital counseling (Fawcitt et al., 2010).

Cohabiting couples live in relationships that are committed and are very similar to marriage. Single adults may still benefit by learning what factors to look for in a mate. The skills taught in this book are meant to help couples have successful relationships regardless of whether or not they marry.

Myth #4: Pre-marital counseling will ensure couples will not divorce.

Reality: Marriage is a lot of work. While pre-marital counseling does give a couple better odds of preventing divorce, it will not do the entire trick. Even in states such as Louisiana where couples have the option to do a more rigorous marital training course called Covenant Marriage, these couples had similar rates of decline in marital satisfaction as other couples who received little or no pre-marital counseling (DeMaris, Sanchez, and Krivickas, 2012). Clinicians need to guide couples to make a long-term plan for what they will do when the marriage gets rough. This plan can include when to go into therapy, marriage enrichment courses along the way, and even preparing couples with the expectation that their marriage will not always be good. Some of the best advice I received before my own marriage, which I now share with my clients and in this book, is "In marriage, you have good days and bad days, good weeks and bad weeks, good years and bad years. Work through them all together."

Myth #5: Clinicians are responsible for teaching couples everything they need to know about marriage.

Reality: It's your responsibility to give them the best knowledge that is available. This book offers a framework for how to teach that knowledge. Ultimately, the couple is responsible for what information they retain and apply throughout their marriage. Your job is to guide them and encourage them to continue to grow. The rest is up to them. You are not responsible for the couple's divorce, should it happen. Marriage is a tough road to navigate for any person, including therapists.

How to Approach this Book

You will learn five habits that promote healthy relationships. These habits stem from years of research in the field of Marriage and Family Therapy. It is primarily systemic in nature in that marriage is viewed as a system in which each partner plays a role (Watzlawick et al., 2011). The individual does not exist in a vacuum. Therefore, one cannot make a decision without it somehow impacting the other person. From this systemic theory, clinicians are given tools to help this system function well.

Clinicians can apply the lessons learned to offer pre-marital counseling in a fun, approachable way. It provides a step-by-step guide for how clinicians can create a pre-marital program that is both informative and addresses couple's individual needs through counseling. However, this book also relies on the clinician's expertise to recognize and attend to the couples who need more intensive therapy. This book does not go extensively into specific issues such as intimate partner violence, substance abuse, or other potentially harmful behaviors. Use best judgment and offer further resources should the relationship appear to be potentially harmful or require more than the basic eight sessions suggested in this book.

This book provides a basic understanding of the habits necessary for a healthy relationship, along with specific skills to teach clients how to perfect these habits. The habits discussed are designed to be informative and to encourage clinicians to incorporate skills already learned from other models of therapy. In essence, this book is a model from which clinicians can build their own pre-marital plans.

The book's order is written to what a typical eight-session pre-marital plan would start with: assessment and treatment planning (session 1), the five healthy habits (sessions 2–6), a chapter dedicated to individualized problems (session 7), and termination of treatment (session 8). However, the chapters in this book can be read and applied out of order, as determined by the couple's needs.

For some clinicians, the skills included will be reviews of older ideas. For newer clinicians, the skills will offer new and unique perspectives for how to teach the habits listed in the book. For all clinicians, this book will provide an engaging format to teach the lessons we know about healthy marriages. Marriage is a system of habits: given practice, couples can achieve a healthy and satisfying long-term relationship.

Bibliography

Beachcombing (2011). How to choose your bride in the late 19th century. *Beachcombing's Bizarre History Blog*, www.strangehistory.net/2011/11/23/how-to-choose-your-bride-in-the-late-nineteenth-century.

Campbell, K. and Wright, D.W. (2010). Marriage Today: Exploring the Incongruence between Americans' Beliefs and Practices. *Journal of Comparative Family Studies, 41*(3), 329–345.

Carroll, J.S. and Doherty, W.J. (2003). Evaluating the effectiveness of premarital prevention programs: A meta-analytic review of outcome research. *Family Relations, 52*, 105–118.

Celello, K. (2009). *Making Marriage Work: A History of Marriage and Divorce in the Twentieth-Century United States*. NC: University of North Carolina Press.

Coontz, S. (2005). *Marriage, A History: How Love Conquered Marriage*. New York: Viking.

DeMaris, A., Sanchez, L.A., and Krivickas, K. (2012). Developmental patterns in marital satisfaction: Another look at covenant marriage. *Journal of Marriage and Family, 74*, 989–1004.

Duncan, S.F., Childs, G.R., and Larson, J.H. (2010). Perceived helpfulness of four different types of marriage preparation interventions. *Family Relations, 59*(5), 623–636.

Fawcitt, E.B., Hawkins, A.J., Blanchard, V.L., and Carroll, J.S. (2010). Do premarital education programs really work? A meta-analytic study. *Family Relations, 59*(3), 232–239.

Fortenberry, J. and Heckerling, A. (1998). *A Night at the Roxbury*. Paramount Pictures.

Gottman, J. (1995). *Why Marriages Succeed or Fail*. New York: Simon & Shuster.

Horton, R.F. (2009). *On the Art of Living Together*. Charleston, SC: Bibliolife. Reprinted edition.

King, M.P. (2008). *Sex and the City*. New Line Cinema.

Parker-Pope, T. (2010). Seeking to Pre-empt Marital Strife. *The New York Times*, http://well.blogs.nytimes.com/2010/06/28/seeking-to-pre-empt-marital-strife/comment-page-7/?_r=0.

Tartakovsky, M. (2012). A Glimpse into Marriage Advice in the 1950s. *PsychCentral*, http://psychcentral.com/blog/archives/2012/02/27/a-glimpse-into-marriage-advice-from-the-1950s.

Watzlawick, P., Weakland, J.H., Fisch, R., Erickson, M.H., and O'Hanlon, B. (2011). *Change: Principles of Problem Formation and Problem Resolution*. New York: W.W. Norton.

Session One

ASSESSMENT AND TREATMENT PLANNING

Before you do anything, be clear of why you want to do it. The purpose is an important reason to support what you'll do.

Sean Penn, *All the King's Men*

The minute a client enters the therapy room, clinicians have a lot of work to do. Not only are clinicians responsible for giving the best advice, but we have to assess for potential problems, interaction patterns, and client willingness to change.

This chapter will focus on the different areas in a pre-marital couple's life that a clinician should assess for in the first session. You will learn various factors that contribute to marital success and typical challenges new couples will face when planning for marriage. You will also learn about some of the most commonly used professional assessments available should you choose to incorporate these into your pre-marital treatment program.

Once you have learned how to properly assess your pre-marital clients, you will then learn how to incorporate that assessment into a treatment plan that is individualized for your client. The purpose of pre-marital counseling is to help couples work through any issues they may be struggling with before getting married. In the case of couples who are not having any issues, the purpose of pre-marital counseling is to identify potential problem areas that could become issues later in marriage and to give couples tools to create a healthy, happy marriage.

Getting Their Story

Matthew and Jenna have come for their first pre-marital session. They are eager to learn all about marriage as they are preparing for their own wedding. Matthew is an engineer. He works 60 to 70 hours weekly and often travels. Jenna, a manager for a retail store, tends to work 40 hours weekly on evenings and weekends. They met 4 years ago in college during a fraternity party and have been together ever since.

When a couple like this is in session, your first goal is to get to know all you can about the clients. Questions to ask your clients include:

1. How did you first meet?
2. What do you want most from pre-marital counseling?
3. How did you decide to get married?
4. Who popped the question, when and how?
5. When is the wedding? What is the wedding plan so far?

A key component to the first session is building a trusting relationship with your clients. The research on the most common factors of successful treatment states that the therapeutic alliance accounts for 30 percent of treatment outcomes (Sprenkle and Blow, 2007). In the first session, the main focus should be on creating a trusting therapeutic relationship. By the end of the session, you should have a clear idea of the client's goals for treatment, a general knowledge of each client's background, and some ideas for what types of tools will be most helpful to address with your clients.

Predictive Factors for Marital Success

In addition to building a therapeutic alliance, clinicians need to assess for critical factors that predict marital stability. Critical factors or predictors can be found during pre-marital relationship formation and development (Fischer and Corcoran, 1994). These pre-marital predictors include background and contextual factors, individual traits and behaviors, and couple interactional processes (Larson et al., 1995).

The first predictor, background and contextual factors, can include many things: family of origin, expectations and values about marriage, race, education, socioeconomic background, and support from friends and family (Larson et al., 2002). In order to assess background and contextual factors, here are some examples of questions you may ask:

1. Are your families (i.e. parents and siblings) similar or different? In what ways?
2. Do you feel comfortable with your new in-laws or are there problems?
3. Do you feel as though they are supportive of your choice to marry one another? If not, how is this affecting your plans currently? Do you feel you have other supports such as friends?
4. What are your beliefs about marriage? What does your ideal marriage look like?
5. Do you both have similar incomes, work history, etc.?
6. Do you believe you both should work or do you prefer alternative roles such as one person staying home while the other works?

The second predictor, individual traits and behaviors, refers to self-esteem, personal hygiene and health habits, personality traits, and an individual's temperament or ability to deal with stressful emotions (Larson et al., 1995, 2002). For each individual in counseling, a clinician should assess for mental illness, disability, or problematic behaviors such as alcohol and drug abuse. In addition to this, the clinician should assess for personality differences. In order to assess individual traits and behaviors, here are some examples of questions you may ask:

1. Do you consider yourself more of an introvert or an extrovert? Explain.
2. How do you two handle household chores? Do you have a system in place?
3. Do you value living an active lifestyle or a more passive one? Do you feel you both are similar in terms of the foods you like, exercise habits, and relaxation habits?

4. Have either of you ever been in counseling prior to today? What were you in counseling for? Did you receive a diagnosis?
5. What are your drinking/smoking habits? Are you similar or different regarding these habits?
6. How well do you think you handle conflict in general?

The third predictor, couple interactional processes, includes how well a couple communicates and resolves conflict, similarities in how to address values, religion, money, and various issues the couple may experience in life as a team (Larson et al., 2002). Some of the top areas that your couples are likely to need to discuss include money, sex, values and expectations, parenting/co-parenting, religion/personal beliefs about right and wrong, politics, use of free time, and work. In order to assess a couple's interaction processes, here are some examples of questions you may ask:

1. How do you two handle a disagreement?
2. How similar are your values and beliefs? If they are different, how often do these differences come up? How do you find a way to work through these differences?
3. How similar are your views on life? Politics? Religion/spirituality?
4. Do you plan to have children?
5. What are your life goals?
6. What type of financial backgrounds did you come from? What are your views about saving, spending, and budgeting?

Sometime during your assessment session, ask your clients about their goals for pre-marital counseling. This information will help you to tailor your pre-marital plan to fit your clients' needs.

Professional Assessment Tools

There are many professional assessment tools available for use. While some clinicians prefer to do their own individual assessment, others may prefer to use a more professional assessment. In this section, we will focus on the top three most popular and accurate assessments available: PREPARE, RELATE and FOCUS.

There are many benefits to using a standardized assessment. First, these assessments have been designed to assess pre-marital relationships. Second, the tests listed here are comprehensive and include at least 75 percent of the predictive qualities of a successful marriage. Third, they are easy to use. Fourth, they are relatively easy to interpret. Fifth, the tests have already been proven to be both reliable and valid (Larson et al., 1995). In addition to the above benefits, it may also be easier to use an assessment that is already created to guide your treatment. There are many factors that may be relevant to address with the couple that could be missed without the use of a standardized test.

In addition to advantages, some disadvantages occur using the professional assessments. In Rowden, Harris, and Stahmann's (2006) testing of the use of one assessment in a group setting, group leaders noticed couples may have taken the test too seriously. While some couples may gain a lot from doing a pre-marital inventory, other couples may see it as potentially predictive of the relationship's doom. In various studies discussing the assessments listed below, researchers stated that the assessment can be used as a helpful tool to guide clinicians in which way to focus treatment (Larson et al., 1995; Williams and Jurich, 1995; Rowden, Harris, and Stahmann, 2006). However, some couples may believe that they have no hope if they do not score very well on such a test. It would be important for the clinician to reframe a bad score to a couple as an opportunity for them to grow as a team.

Some clinicians and clients may also feel that it limits where pre-marital education can go. For example, clients may feel the clinician relies too heavily on the assessment and does not address the goals they feel are most important. Clinicians may feel that it limits their own creative capacity within the therapeutic context. To prevent this from happening, the clinician should always defer to their clients' goals for pre-marital counseling. This way, the clients are given the control of the sessions and clinicians can guide sessions according to their client's wishes.

PREPARE

The PREPARE assessment is commonly used by clinicians for pre-marital counseling. The PREPARE assessment addresses "10 core scales that include the following: communication, conflict resolution, financial management, leisure activities, sexual relationship, role relationship, spiritual beliefs, personality issues, parenting, family and friends" (Olson, 2015, p. 3). It is included as one of three of the assessments reviewed by Larson et al. (2002) and was considered comprehensive. In addition, it is shorter in length than some of the other assessments available.

Clinicians interested in using this assessment can find it at www. prepare-enrich.com. Couples taking this test should go to the couples section of the website for more information. This particular assessment does require some training for the clinician. Clinicians can either take a local one-day training at around $175 in their area or they can do an online training course for $225. During the training clinicians are taught how to offer the assessment, discuss the results, and use the results to shift their pre-marital treatment for clients. This assessment also comes with treatment tools that can be used.

RELATE

The RELATE Inventory is an assessment that is commonly used by clinicians for pre-marital counseling. "RELATE's conceptual model is based on over 50 years of research regarding important premarital predictors that reflect later marital quality and stability" (Rowden, Harris, and Stahmann, 2006, p. 49). It looks at four main categories: 1) personality characteristics, 2) similarity of values, 3) family background, and 4) relationship experiences. It is also one of five pre-marital assessment questionnaires (PAQs) that are considered comprehensive since it includes at least 96 percent of the pre-marital factors that predict marital quality (Larson et al., 1995).

For clinicians interested in this assessment, it is relatively easy to access and use. The assessment can be found at www.relate-institute.org. Couples can be guided to go to the participant section to begin their own assessment. The cost is $20 per person and the assessment generates a 20-page report that can be printed out. There is no cost to the clinician to use the service.

Clinicians can also sign up for RELATE rather easily. There is no formal training to offer the assessment. Clinicians must complete the online professional application and prove they are a trained professional. They will be asked to offer documentation such as licensure. After getting credentialed, it is relatively easy to use. Clinicians can opt to have their clients' questionnaires sent to them as well for use in pre-marital counseling.

FOCCUS

FOCCUS is a pre-marital counseling assessment that is also available. It offers several questions that assess the strengths and potential areas of growth for couples. It was originally designed for the Catholic population but has since expanded to include both Christian and non-religious populations. It is developed to help a wide variety of couples including two-career, teen, interfaith, and second marriages (Williams and Jurich, 1995).

It is also considered comprehensive by Larson et al. (1995) in that it covers at least 78 percent of the predictive factors of marital satisfaction. The assessment has even been used in follow-up studies at 5 years after marriage to consider how closely the test predicts marital success. FOCCUS is also offered in six languages and six versions.

To become familiar with FOCCUS, clinicians can visit their website at www.foccusinc.com. There are two training courses available for clinicians to get certified to use the assessment. Clinicians can either take a one-day training course with a local trainer or do online training on their own. Once trained, you can register to use the instrument and have your clients go directly to the website to complete their assessment. The cost for couples is $15 or $10 for an individual.

Treatment Planning

After assessing the different client issues, clinicians can create a treatment plan. The key to effective treatment planning is to personalize the treatment plan to fit your clients' needs. In this book, I offer suggestions for how to run a pre-marital counseling program that lasts from six to eight sessions. The typical treatment plan should include one assessment session, five sessions that focus on the five habits for successful marriages, and two optional sessions that focus more specifically on issues that couples may need to address prior to marriage. An example is now given.

Pre-marital Treatment Plan

Session 1: Assessment and Treatment Planning—Learn about couple's goals, assess for potential issues, and create a customized treatment plan. Reading: TBA.

Session 2: Choosing to Love—Couples learn how to actively choose to love in their relationships. Reading: TBA.

Session 3: Being Empathetic—Couples learn about differences in their communication styles so they can be more validating partners. Reading: TBA.

Session 4: Fighting Respectfully—Couples learn some helpful skills for how to reduce or prevent conflict in their relationship. Reading: TBA.

Session 5: Asking for Needs and Wants Effectively—Couples learn how to use a positive approach to meet their needs. Reading: TBA.

Session 6: Keeping the Spark Alive—Couples discuss any sexual concerns, learn about common sexual problems, and learn specific ideas for keeping the spark alive in their relationship long term. Reading: TBA.

Session 7: Specific Client Issues. Reading: TBA.

Session 8: Specific Client Issues and Termination. Reading: TBA.

Therapist Signature   Date

The treatment plan above gives an overall guideline for how pre-marital counseling will run. Based on the assessment in the first session, a clinician may add more specific ideas for each session. For sessions 2 through 6, I typically pick one or two interventions from the chapters associated with the main topic. These interventions can be found in the corresponding chapters later in this book. For sessions 7 and 8, I leave room for specific issues the clients may need to address.

Homework assignments help your clients feel as though they are getting more out of therapy. I encourage you to look for articles or videos that are relevant to each session. I always print out the articles myself and give them to clients. Videos on YouTube are also a good option as there are now many TED talks (an online forum) offered for free online by professional counselors and people in many professions. Find out which types of homework your clients prefer: videos or articles. This way, clients are more likely to follow through with homework assignments.

I encourage you to read your treatment plans out loud to your clients at the start of the second session and give them a copy to take home. This gives clients a chance to discuss the plan and ask for any additional sessions if needed. It will also give you a chance to make sure you are covering the issues they want to address.

Giving Clients Hope

I was at a networking event for women. I stood in a group of three women and told them I was interested in finding couples who are successfully married for at least 10 years. One woman stated her husband recently passed from cancer. The other woman stated she was recently divorced. The other woman said she had been married for 40 years—30 good, but the last few years had been rough.

Earlier in that same day, I stood before a group of men and women at a different networking group trying to find the couples successfully married. Interestingly, it was other people who suggested friends. People did not volunteer themselves. One guy stated, "Hey, Jay, you've been married for over 30 years." He was hesitant to reply.

I realized that couples are struggling with this topic. Couples have a real fear about whether or not their relationship is healthy. Even people who are in marriages that have lasted many years still sometimes question whether or not they are getting the most out of their marriages or if they are even happy. The truth? Success in marriage is relative. There are times when marriages are happy and times when people question their marriages. In many ways, this is common.

As clinicians, we need to do our best to normalize fears and establish hope for the couples who come to us for pre-marital counseling. It's okay to worry about a future marriage. People divorce around us every day. The couples that you think are the happiest sometimes end unexpectedly. It is scary to be married at times and to trust that your relationship is okay.

When clients discuss these fears with you, learn to encourage hope. In the common factors literature, hope is one of the predictors of success in counseling (Sprenkle and Blow, 2007). Offer hope by giving your clients positive feedback about all the things they already are doing well. Over the next few weeks, use those strengths to encourage growth.

Practice Ideas

1. Look up articles and videos that relate to the various pre-marital topics we address in this book such as fair fighting, empathy, marital expectations, etc. If you find reader-friendly articles or videos, suggest your clients read these in between sessions.
2. Practice making your own pre-marital treatment plans using the skills you learn in this book.
3. Go to one of the seminars that train you to use a professional assessment tool. See if this assessment would help guide your pre-marital counseling.

Bibliography

Busby, D.M., Ivey, D.C., Harris, S.M., and Ates, C. (2007). Self-directed, therapist directed, and assessment based interventions for premarital couples. *Family Relations, 56*, 279–290.

Fischer, J. and Corcoran, K. (1994). *Measures for clinical practice: A sourcebook. Vol. 1, Couples, families and children*, 2nd ed. New York: The Free Press.

Larson, J.H., Newell, K., Topham, G., and Nichols, S. (2002). A review of three comprehensive premarital assessment questionnaires. *Journal of Marital and Family Therapy, 28*(2), 233–239.

Larson, J.H., Holman, T.B., Klein, D.M., Busby, D.M., Stahmann, R.F., and Peterson, D. (1995). A review of comprehensive questionnaires used in premarital education and counseling. *Family Relations, 44*, 245–252.

Olson, D.H. (2015). 10 ways couple assessment can improve any relationship education program. *Life Innovations*, 1–5.

Rowden, T.J., Harris, S.M., and Stahmann, R.F. (2006). Group premarital counseling using a premarital assessment questionnaire: Evaluation from group leaders. *The American Journal of Family Therapy, 34*, 47–61.

Sprenkle, D.H. and Blow, A.J. (2007; first published 2004). Common factors and our sacred models. *Journal of Marital and Family Therapy, 3*(2), 113–129.

TED talks (2015). TED Conferences, LLC.

Williams, L. and Jurich, J. (1995). Predicting marital success after five years: Assessing the predictive validity of FOCCUS. *Journal of Marital and Family Therapy, 21*(2), 141–153.

Zaillian, S. (2006). *All the King's Men*. Sony Pictures.

Session Two

CHOOSING TO LOVE

We're all a little weird. And life is a little weird. And when we find someone whose weirdness is compatible with ours, we join up with them and fall into mutually satisfying weirdness—and call it love—true love.

Robert Fulghum, *True Love*

In 1997, *Titanic* was one of the most popular love stories. A young woman and a young man met, two strangers on a ship that was destined to sink. The main character, Rose, was a rich woman promised to another rich man. She meets Jack, a poor man who teaches her how to love and enjoy life again. Toward the end of the movie, they are madly in love and ready to die together in the cold, dark waters. The problem with this scenario—they only knew each other for about a week. Perhaps in 5 years, after Rose lived in squalor with her lover, she might not have been as keen to die in cold waters with him. Anyone who has been in love long term knows that the intense feeling at the beginning of a relationship changes over time. Married love is work.

The honeymoon phase in a relationship is a well-documented phenomenon. This phase starts in the beginning of the relationship and lasts up to 2 years. "This period features high levels of passionate love, characterized by intense feelings of attraction and ecstasy, as well as an idealization of one's partner" (Lewandowski, 2013, p. 1). It is easy to love your partner during the honeymoon phase, but it takes work to show that same level of love over time. The first habit for successful marriages is to work intentionally to keep your love strong.

What kind of work does long-term love require? For couples to maintain their love, they need to choose to love their partner every day. Loving is a verb, which means there are actions each partner needs to take that will ensure that their partner feels loved and they feel loved in return. After the honeymoon period, couples can still feel romantic about each other, but they need to understand that the feeling won't always come naturally. The day-to-day responsibilities of life can get in the way of that feeling and if they don't put effort into loving their partner, that feeling can die.

Myths about Love

There are many myths regarding love that invade our consciousness daily. These myths come from the media, friends, families, and greater culture. The challenge as clinicians is to dispel these myths in a way that encourages couples to create the best possible marriages.

In a recent study, 86 percent of people married or single, aged 18 to 29 expect their marriage to last a lifetime (Lotze, 2012) despite the fact that 50 percent of marriages end in divorce. At the beginning of a relationship, most couples expect their marriage to last forever. Couples have less negative history with each other, typically are getting along, and are still very much in love with each other. One important goal in pre-marital counseling for clinicians is to help set realistic expectations for newly-weds about what love looks like over time.

Myth #1: Married love is butterflies, daffodils, and excitement for the rest of your lives.

Reality: Married love has moments of good and bad. There are two components to the love we experience—infatuation and attachment. Attachment refers to the more comforting feeling of emotional bonding with another individual that can be felt with friends, family, a partner or spouse, while infatuation refers to passionate love or attraction that is typically felt for a lover or partner (Langeslag, Muris, and Franken, 2013). In married love, couples experience attachment love most often, while infatuation comes and goes. Couples who expect to constantly feel "in love" or feel "butterflies" will likely be unhappy with the outcome of married love since it requires work to create the feelings associated with being "in love."

Myth #2: If you are married to the right person, marriage should be easy.

Reality: Some marriages are no doubt easier than other marriages. However, it is not likely that a marriage will be easy all the time. People live very long lives that are bound to come with both positive and negative situations. Clinicians need to remind their clients that when things aren't going well, this does not necessarily mean their relationship is in a bad spot. During times of difficulty, clients need guidance about how to remain close and stay connected. Sometimes this requires more work.

For example, Jim and Susan had met when they were in college. They had been married for 20 years. They still both loved each other, but they had a very hard road recently. Over the last 3 years, both their biological parents had died, Susan had gotten cancer, and Jim had to take care of her through her chemotherapy. The constant stress had put a strain on their marriage. Instead of feeling close, they were being more snippy and rude at times. This couple would definitely report they had married the right person, but marriage had become a challenge for other reasons.

Myth #3: Once you've lost that loving feeling, you can't fall back in love with your spouse.

Given that there are two different types of love, attachment and romantic love, many couples experience times in their life when they say, "I love you, but I am not in love with you." In the article "The Science of Love" (BBC, 2014), the author describes three distinct stages of love including Lust—sexual interest and desire, Attraction—lovestruck and fully enamored with their partner, and Attachment—which refers to the long-term commitment bond. When partners say they have fallen out of love, they are often referring to the transition from lust and attraction to a more attachment-based love. Couples who expect these first stages to remain as intense throughout their lives are in for a shock. Sometimes when couples transition, they think they have fallen out of love with their partner.

However, it is common for couples who have been married for many years to have times where they feel more or less loving toward their partner. For example, Henry and Lydia had gotten into the habit of doing everything for their children. As their children became teenagers, they started to get more time with each other and realized they had lost that old spark they used to feel for one another. That year, they spent a lot of time dating each other and putting effort into their romantic relationship. Essentially they had to get to know each other in a brand new way in order to fall back in love romantically. They had to put more conscious effort into showing love toward each other. After that year, they reported they loved each other more than they ever had.

Myth #4: Married love is boring.

Reality: Married love is different, but that does not mean it has to be boring. When couples commit to sharing their lives, they are committing to the good and the bad: the new experiences and the mundane experiences. They are committing to who their partner is currently, and who and how their partner will change over time. In a typical life cycle, couples will experience several basic life cycle transitions including being newly married, raising children, guiding children through adolescence, launching of adult children, and lives as older adults (Carter and McGoldrick, 1989). In addition to these basic transitions, couples will also experience job loss and changes, relocation, and as we age, disability and illness. Marriage, like life, is what a person makes of it. People can choose to have a boring life or choose to live their lives to the fullest, married or single.

Myth #5: Love will complete you.

Reality: In many fairy tales growing up, the underlying message to young women was to find a Prince Charming and live happily ever after. While love is great, it is only a part of a couple's marriage. The other part people don't often discuss is the business of marriage. The business of marriage includes the To-Do List, the chores, the appointment making, the settling of affairs, and the co-parenting. Sometimes, if a couple is not good at negotiating the business of their marriage, their love doesn't seem to be strong enough.

In Margot Peppers' (2013) article featuring the artistic work of Dina Goldstein, the Disney princesses are depicted in real-life situations such as Snow White with her unemployed prince husband raising four kids, or Rapunzel who loses her long, beautiful hair during chemotherapy. Dina's art depicts the business of marriage or the day-to-day life struggles. It strikes a hard contrast to the Disney themes that suggest that true love will complete a person. The reality is that marriage is both times of happiness and times of struggle. As Patty Smyth (1992) says in her famous song, "Sometimes love just ain't enough."

There are times in a couple's relationship when they need to rely on themselves and their own happiness. In some ways, couples getting married do experience some important benefits such as "intimacy, companionship, and day-to-day interaction, and they connect their partners to larger networks of friends, kin, and community that can be drawn on in times of need" (Musick and Bumpass, 2012, p. 2). In other ways, an individual's happiness or completeness is based in part on their own baseline of happiness. For example, researchers looked at levels of happiness before and after marriage. They found an initial boost in happiness right after marriage followed by a return to baseline happiness after a brief honeymoon period (Lucas et al., 2003). In general, marriage alone does not necessarily improve a person's self-esteem or sense of wholeness. It is their personal choices, level of health, and general happiness that will contribute to feelings of wholeness.

How to Teach your Clients to Love

There are two helpful concepts about love in romantic relationships— showing love and accepting love. On the one hand, love is an action that a person takes to show the way they feel about another person. A person may show love by giving a kiss, saying "I love you," or doing something kind for another person. In this way, love is a verb. On the other hand, love also requires acceptance. A person may accept the love they are given by receiving that kiss with open arms, responding to someone's "I love you" with an accepting smile, or genuinely thanking that person for their kindness. In pre-marital counseling, clinicians are responsible for teaching clients a very important habit—how to actively participate in love, accept the love they are given, and create a love that can grow over time.

Couple Rituals

A couple ritual is an act or behavior that a couple participates in consistently. Couple rituals can include brushing teeth together as a couple, kissing before leaving for work and when coming back from work, dancing in the kitchen while waiting for the water to boil, scratching a partner's back before bed, etc. One couple, Jana and Kevin, would sway together holding each other in the kitchen. Another couple, Darren and Michael would sit together on their porch every night before bed, watch the sunset, and talk about their day.

I have often noticed that when couples come into marriage therapy with problems, they are not participating in the rituals that once made them happy. One partner will say, "You used to cuddle with me before bed" or "You never call me sweetheart anymore." Part of rebuilding their relationship is often to help them begin to insert new couple rituals or bring old rituals back that helped them feel close.

In pre-marital counseling, clinicians can guide couples in either recognizing the rituals they already use or in creating new ones to include. The session can start by asking your clients questions such as, "What couple rituals do you currently use or have you seen other couples use?" If the couple has some trouble figuring out what to do, you can teach them the five love languages to get some ideas. In the book *The Five Love Languages,* Gary Chapman (2009) outlines five different ways couples can show love to one another through time, touch, words of affirmation, acts of service, and gifts. If including this information in the session, clinicians can write the five love languages up on the board and ask clients to identify specific couple rituals they would enjoy from their partner under each category.

Once they have come up with their own list, encourage each of them to practice actively participating in one or more rituals daily. This can remind clients that choosing to love is a daily activity. It's not something one does every now and then when they remember to do so. To truly build a lasting love, each individual must learn to choose to love their partner each day in some way even when it has been a rough day. In fact, during rough days, couples need to work harder to show love because that is when people need it the most.

Sharing Positive Memories

Charles and Doris, my grandparents, have been married for over 60 years. While recalling an old fight between them, Charles remembered saying, "You go home to your mother!" She replied, "You talk silly, we are married!" He then said with a smile, "I shut up right after that. She was much smarter than me."—Compliments of Doris and Charles Marshall.

Have you ever sat with an older couple and listened to their stories? With the happiest couples, they tend to tell either funny memories or recall sweet memories. They almost always have an air of nostalgia around them and smiles on their faces. When a couple shares a positive memory, it brings back old feelings of connection and happiness. John Gottman (1995) reported that couples need a ratio of five positive interactions to one negative interaction. Sharing positive memories is one active tool couples can use to experience a positive connection.

Clinicians can guide clients to restate old positive memories as a skill to bring back feelings of joy, connection, and positivity. To use this skill in session, clinicians can ask clients to discuss one or more memories. If your clients struggle to figure one out, you can offer ideas such as the first date, the first time they knew they loved their partner, or an embarrassing moment they shared but can both laugh about now.

Clinicians should discuss with their couples how they can use this skill in different points in their lives. For example, some couples can start a memory conversation when they are feeling somewhat distant from their partner. Other couples may choose to take time weekly or monthly to discuss old positive memories. Guide your couples in deciding what works best for them.

Appreciations

In the popular television show *It's Always Sunny in Philadelphia*, Season 8, Episode 1 (2012), Charlie is in love with the waitress. He typically follows her around and protects her from many potential problems. However, in this episode he stops doing things to help her at her request. By the end of the episode, the waitress has been attacked by someone who broke into her house, had her bike stolen, and lost some of her hair. She begs Charlie to come back and keep her safe, even if still at a distance.

In the above story, the waitress struggles to accept the love she is given by Charlie because she sees it as overbearing and stalker-like. Technically, he is her stalker in the show. However, in many normal relationships, individuals try to show love to their partners and feel their efforts go unnoticed and/or unreciprocated. Clinicians can teach clients how to recognize and accept the love they are given by teaching the appreciation skill.

There are two ways to teach the appreciation skill. The first method is more active and should involve both clients. Have each client list five or more things they appreciated from their partner this week. You can then encourage each partner to take turns sharing their lists with each other. Periodically, couples can use this same skill at times when they are feeling under-appreciated by each other in their marriage.

As a second method, each partner can be encouraged to pay attention to all the ways their partner has showed love to them over the week. As they notice love actions they appreciate, they can encourage their partner's action with comments such as, "Thank you for giving me that hug" or "you made me feel so loved when you did the dishes for me." Basically, clinicians can teach couples to positively reinforce behaviors in their partner they appreciate. The one benefit is that people tend to repeat behaviors they feel are appreciated.

Clinicians can encourage clients to use this skill when they find themselves feeling very negative about their partner for a long period of time. Examples of negative thoughts they may have include, "He's always a jerk," or "she never listens," or "he doesn't care about my opinions." When a client's thoughts consistently point to the negative, it can be hard for them to be patient, respectful, and/or kind to their partner. Actively looking for the positive in the relationship can help an individual change the way they view their relationship.

Rookie Mistakes

Some couples may have different expectations about love and what it should look like. For example, John and Dana described love very differently in session. John stated he felt the feelings of love and connection very strongly in the beginning of their relationship. He was looking for the feelings of closeness, the spark of excitement, and the flutter of joy that love brings. His wife-to-be, Dana, had a very different opinion. She saw those first feelings as immature love. She stated love was about being there for each other through hard times and helping each other out.

When couples have different opinions, it is good to validate both of their ideas. Once you have modeled how to validate, it can be helpful to encourage each person to validate or try to understand their partner's opinion. You may guide Dana to see the value in those romantic butterfly feelings while also guiding John to see the value in Dana's attachment-oriented love. At the end of the session, you could encourage each person to come up with one thing they could do to build each style of love.

Another potential challenge is to help couples who do not fall into the hetero-normative category. For example, Tina and Amy struggle with what love should look like in a lesbian relationship. They both stated that the vast majority of relationship models they see are heterosexual couples. This posed a challenge to them because they were unsure at times what roles they should play. Who should be the initiator or planner? How should they divide household tasks? Would their love be stronger or even look the same?

As clinicians, it can be helpful to normalize the challenge lesbian and gay couples face in creating their own models. One thing I try to do is to reframe this challenge into a positive. *Reframing* is a skill from Strategic therapy that involves redefining a situation or behavior emphasizing the positive aspects (Nichols and Schwartz, 2006). For example, while heterosexual couples have models for how to run their relationships, any of these models can still end in divorce. Tina and Amy are in a position to create their own relationship model.

While they can learn from heteronormative models, they don't have to feel forced into specific roles. They have the opportunity to regularly negotiate the rules of their relationship. In heterosexual couples, sometimes certain activities are expected without discussion. These expectations can cause fights. For Tina and Amy, there are no expectations about who should do what. Instead, they can be clear and fair with each other and negotiate the best possible solutions.

A third example of a couple who struggles with love is Michael and Dana. Michael and Dana have been married and divorced. They currently are getting married the second time to each other. While they love each other very much, they are both very fearful that they could fail at this marriage. Michael states, "I sometimes worry that I am going to ruin this relationship too. I don't want to make the same mistakes."

It is common for couples getting married for their second time to enter pre-marital counseling. One encouragement I offer to clients in this place is to remind them of the fact that they are in counseling to make better decisions this time. I typically will ask a client to consider what they have learned from their first marriage about relationships and about themselves. I try to encourage clients to think about things they could have done better in the first marriage. I ask questions such as, "What do you know now that you wish you knew then?" "What will you need to do to make sure this relationship does succeed?" "What is different about the person you are currently marrying?" These questions help clients take personal responsibility for their new marriage and the work they will need to put into their new love.

For any challenges couples face dealing with love, the best course of action is guiding your clients in a conversation about their fears, expectations, and personal responsibilities. While love is work, it is a truly rewarding work. It is one step in building a healthy, long-lasting marriage.

Practice Ideas

1. Read *The Five Love Languages*, by Gary Chapman. See whether some of these ideas may be helpful to include while you teach this session.
2. Take a look at models of healthy marriage in your own life. What common traits do you see among these couples? What common traits do you see among couples who are struggling?
3. Learn about the various attachment styles—Secure, Preoccupied, Dismissive, and Fearful. How could information about attachment help you guide couples to create a more healthy love life? If you

are interested in this area, you may choose to read books associated with Emotion-focused Therapy.

Bibliography

BBC (2014). The Science of Love. *Science: Human Body and Mind*. BBC Homepage, July 4, www.bbc.co.uk/science/hottopics/love.

Cameron, J. (1997). *Titanic*. 20th Century Fox Film Corporation.

Carter, B. and McGoldrick, M. (1989). *The Changing Family Life Cycle: A Framework for Family Therapy*, 2nd ed. Boston: Allyn and Bacon.

Chapman, G. (2009). *The Five Love Languages*. Chicago, IL: Northfield Publishing.

Fulghum, R. (1998). *True Love*. New York: Harper Paperbacks.

Gottman, J. (1995). *Why Marriages Succeed or Fail*. New York: Simon & Shuster.

Langeslag, S.J.E., Muris, P., and Franken, I.H.A. (2013) Measuring romantic love: Psychometric properties of the infatuation and attachment scales. *Journal of Sex Research*, *50*(8), 739–747.

Lewandowski, G.W. (2013). What physiological changes can explain the honeymoon phase of a relationship? *Scientific American*, www.scientificamerican.com/article/what-physiological-changes-can-explain-honeymoon-phase-relationship.

Lotze, K. (2012). Marriage expectations: Young people expect marriages to last, study says. *The Huffington Post*, August 17.

Lucas, R.E., Georgeellis, Y., Clark, A.E., and Diener, E. (2003). Reexamining adaptation and the set point model of happiness: Reactions to changes in marital status. *Personality and Social Psychology*, *84*, 527–539.

McElhenny, R., Howerton, G., and Day, C. (2012). *It's Always Sunny in Philadelphia*. Season 8, Episode 1. FX station.

Musick, K. and Bumpass, L. (2012). Reexamining the case for marriage: Union formation and changes in well-being. *Journal of Marriage and Family*, *74*(1), 1–18.

Nichols, M.P. and Schwartz, R.C. (2006). *Family Therapy: Concepts and Methods*. Boston, MA: Pearson Education.

Peppers, M. (2013). Snow White's failed marriage, an alcoholic Cinderella and an obese Red Riding Hood: Cynical Photo series shows Disney princesses living unhappily ever after. UK Mail Online, August 6. www.dailymail.co.uk/femail/article-2385475/Dina-Goldsteins-Fallen-Princesses-shows-Disneys-Snow-White-Cinderella-unhappily-after.html.

Smyth, P. and Burtnik, G. (1992). "Sometimes love just ain't enough." Sony/ATV Music Publishing LLC. Warner Chappal Music. Universal Music Publishing Group.

Session Three

BEING EMPATHETIC

Yeah I called her up, she gave me a bunch of crap about me not listening to her, or something, I don't know, I wasn't really paying attention.
Jeff Daniels, *Dumb and Dumber*

There were two different parents who had a child who didn't want to go to school. The first parent got mad at her child and told him, "You are going to school whether you like it or not!" Over time the child continued each morning to have a tantrum that escalated and made it more and more difficult to get her child to school. The second parent took a different approach with her child. When he didn't want to go to school, she asked her son, "What's going on? Is school okay for you?" Her son then melted into tears and stated some kids were calling him names and he didn't want to go. After finding out this information, the mother called the teacher and tried to find a way to help her son feel more comfortable. The teacher worked with the other kids and helped them to start getting along better, and over time, the boy no longer avoided going to school.

Being empathetic is the second habit for successful marriages. In the second example above, the mother was using empathy to work through the problem with her child. In couple relationships, empathy is a very valuable tool for helping individuals hear each other, understand problems more clearly, and come up with solutions that actually solve the problems. Empathy does not resolve all problems in a relationship, but it can reduce the intensity and frequency of arguments. It is an important step in teaching couples to get along with each other better.

Empathy is defined as "the ability to understand what the other is thinking, put oneself in the other's place, and intellectually understand one another's condition without vicariously experiencing their emotions" (Angera and Long, 2006, pp. 3–4). Commonly in therapeutic situations, clinicians will see couples who struggle to feel heard and understood by their partner. One of the most common treatment interventions we use that exists in all models of therapy is some type of empathy training. In this chapter, we will discuss a variety of empathy training interventions that can be used to encourage new couples to relate more effectively as a team.

Myths about Empathy

Since the beginning of counseling, most models in therapy have some degree of empathy training as a part of helping couples understand each other better. Clinicians typically are guided to do the following: ask open-ended questions; take a nonjudgmental approach; not add to what a client is saying or take away from it; gently help a client feel understood and validated. As couple therapy began to evolve, clinicians quickly realized that not only do clients need validation or empathy from their therapist, but even more so, they need empathy from each other.

Nevertheless, there are some myths or discrepancies that exist regarding empathy. These myths exist because as a field we are still learning a great deal about empathy and how it contributes to successful marriages. Good research should in fact change the landscape of our field over time by asking more questions and finding more answers or debunking old answers. At this point in the research, there are a few myths that commonly show up that should be addressed.

Myth #1: You have to agree with your partner to show empathy.

Reality: Showing empathy only requires a person to hear someone's perspective and show a level of understanding about that perspective. For example, I once had a couple who was arguing about whether they should sell their house or not—Stephanie and Darren. Stephanie stated she loved the area where they were building the house and she could not see giving it up. It had been their dream to build a home in Ladue, a prominent community in the St. Louis area. Years ago they had acquired land in the area for a decent price. Darren believed that selling was the best choice because they weren't making as much money in recent years as they were making when they first bought the land. Due to this, they had not even started building a house since they purchased the land.

The couple in the above example can show empathy to work through the disagreement. Darren could show empathy by stating, "I could see why you wouldn't want to sell this house. It really was our dream to build a home here. It must be painful to consider selling it." In this example, he is not necessarily agreeing to keep the house. He is merely stating his understanding of Stephanie's feelings. Stephanie can also show empathy by saying, "I could see why you think selling is the best option. We have been struggling financially for quite some time. That must feel very stressful to not know how we will pay our bills." In this example, Stephanie has not agreed to sell the house, but she has at least showed some compassion for Darren's feelings.

In this example, they each have opened up the discussion by showing some empathy for their partner's ideas. They have shown that they can understand and respect their partner's opinion, even if it is different from their own. Couples need to use empathy to let their partners know they value their judgment and they don't think they are crazy. Using this skill helps individuals lower their defenses so they can begin to negotiate for the best possible solution.

Myth #2: Active listening, also known as empathy training or validation, is required for couples to communicate effectively.

Reality: There is some debate about this topic. Empathy training is commonly used in a variety of therapy models. However, in the research of Gottman et al. (1998), couples rarely used active listening strategies during conflict. Angera and Long's (2006) research suggested that pushing the use of these types of skills may set couples up for unrealistic expectations. However, Long et al. (1999) suggest that couples could be taught how to use empathy to improve their listening skills over time.

I have seen the value of teaching empathy skills to my clients in sessions. Empathy tends to help couples see eye to eye, even when they disagree about the topic matter. How I try to set realistic expectations is by suggesting that couples learn this skill and try their best to use the skill during conflict. However, sometimes couples will get into an argument without using the skills. Even when couples make mistakes, they can cool down and then discuss the situation again using the skills. This way, if the couple fails at using the skills at first, they still have an opportunity to improve the situation after the heat of the moment. I find couples tend to use empathy skills more when they know it is okay to have a few failures along the way. Also, clinicians can improve the use of the skills by having clients practice them in session several times before suggesting they try things at home.

Myth #3: Being empathetic during an argument will help couples resolve conflict.

Reality: This is sometimes the case and sometimes not the case. In some circumstances, a couple's use of empathy will help them to reduce the intensity of an argument. However, an argument is often a high-pressure situation for couples and it is a very difficult time for couples to be empathetic. The very nature of an argument includes raising voices, stating different opinions, and sometimes not listening to or caring about the other person's perspective. An individual is commonly trying to prove their partner wrong during an argument. Empathy in this circumstance may be very difficult or even counterintuitive to the ultimate goal of proving a partner wrong.

I typically suggest that when couples are engaged in an argument, if they find themselves talking over each other or getting nowhere in an argument, to end the discussion until they are ready to be more empathetic and listen to their partner's ideas. I truly believe that empathy is a more valuable skill when it is done day to day in everyday conversation and used after an argument has cooled down. The hope is that over time, with continued use of empathy, couples can shift their style of arguing from trying to prove their partner wrong to trying to understand each other and resolve conflict.

Myth #4: Showing empathy can help couples feel resolution even if they do not come up with specific solutions to the problem.

Reality: Yes and no. In some circumstances, a couple is fighting with a similar resolution in mind. I have often watched couples fight, heard their different perspectives, and realized they actually were agreeing with each other. Since they each were wording things differently and were defensive, they were unable to hear their partner agreeing with them. In cases like these, guiding couples to show empathy can help them recognize that they are in fact agreeing. Once they recognize this, the resolution becomes clear.

A second example of when empathy may be helpful is in cases where there is nothing to actually resolve. Sometimes, couples are discussing feelings of hurt or disappointment. In these cases, all one partner may crave is for their partner to state, "I am sorry you are feeling so sad. I had no idea you felt like that." There is nothing necessarily that he or she can do to fix the feeling for that person. The hurt individual is responsible for pulling themselves out of that feeling. They are sharing the feeling with their partner to feel supported. Often, people miss opportunities to show support because when they hear their partner discuss a feeling, they take it personally or assume it is their responsibility to fix the feeling.

While the above examples show when empathy is helpful, there are times when empathy is not the final step. I have had couples discuss an issue in my office very empathetically understanding each other's point of view, only to still feel discord at the end of the discussion. There are some issues that truly need either a compromise or win/win solution to make them happy going forward. For these couples, clinicians need to guide their couples past the initial empathy into negotiating for best potential outcomes. Empathy will help them to hear each other's ideas better, but they will still need to create a peaceful solution to their problems.

Myth #5: Showing empathy is a weakness and is similar to giving in.

Reality: Typically women are taught how to be more empathetic while men are taught to stand their ground and fight for their rights. When I teach empathy skills, it is commonly men who suggest that empathy is a weakness. I think a big reason for this is how differently men and women are socialized.

The reality is that it takes a lot of work and strength to empathize with someone that you disagree with, especially if it involves a potential outcome that could affect you. In therapy, I am constantly in a position where I am trying to be empathetic when a person is saying things I am vehemently opposed to. However, it is easier for me to be empathetic as a therapist because ultimately my client's decision will have little effect on my life. In my personal life, to empathize with my husband or a friend, empathy is very challenging because my natural response is to fight like hell for my opinion. What I continue to recognize is that fighting in this way gets me no closer to my ultimate resolution. Honestly, it is much harder to practice empathy for someone you disagree with than it is to fight like hell to prove them wrong. In this way, I believe empathy is not a sign of weakness, but a display of great strength and personal self-control.

How to Teach Your Clients Empathy

There are a variety of ways you can teach your clients about empathy. Since empathy skills exist in almost every model of therapy, there are many options to choose from that will help you teach your clients to be more empathetic toward one another. When choosing, you should ask your clients what type of learning style they prefer to use—audio, visual, or tactile. If they are looking for a more tactile approach, you may choose some interventions that require them to practice the skill in session. If you have a client who is more visual, you may select from videos they can watch such as Headley's (2013) internet video "It's not about the Nail." It's important to tailor your treatment to fit your client's learning style.

6 Levels of Validation

Jimmy and Nathan were in therapy to work through problems with Jimmy's daughter Nadine. Nathan always felt as though Jimmy and Nadine made decisions without him. Nathan also reported feeling as though he was left out of decision making within his relationship with Jimmy. During the session, I introduced the "6 Levels of Validation" by Marsha Linehan (Hall, 2015). After having them read the validations, I helped each use validation Level 2 which involves restating their partner's words back to their partner. At the end of the session, Jimmy and Nathan didn't necessarily have the final resolution, but they did feel heard and understood by their partner.

The 6 Levels of Validation is a skill set developed by Marsha Linehan, the founder of Dialectical Behavior Therapy. A good recap can be found at www.blackloveandmarriage.com (Hall, 2015). Since the skill set is usually used to teach therapists how to be more validating, I usually will only teach clients the first two levels of validation. However, this website reframes the levels of validation in such a way that clients could easily understand the concepts as well. You may choose to use them all if you find them helpful.

The first two levels of validation discuss both verbal and non-verbal communication that can be used to convey a level of understanding. Level 1 validation, "Listening and Observing," involves being both verbally and non-verbally present with a partner. An individual is fully focused on what their partner says and is trying to understand their point of view. A person is non-judgmental and tries to be curious and respectful (Linehan, 2015).

Level 2 validation involves restating what the person has said in your own words. A person tries to clearly restate what they think they have heard, to communicate they understand what their partner means. There is no added meaning, no changing the subject, or no guiding the conversation. When a person validates, they are simply trying to state out loud what they think their partner's perspective is.

In order to teach the skill, I usually bring out the first two levels and have clients read it in session. After reading it, I ask clients what areas they personally could improve upon at either Level 1 or 2 validation. Then, I lead the couple in a conversation about how each of them could intentionally improve their ability to show empathy. For couples who prefer a more tactile approach (learning by doing), I will have my clients discuss a lower-level argument in session and have them each practice showing validation to their partner. This is particularly helpful for clients who do not seem to validate their partner well in sessions. As they practice, I give clients suggestions for how they can improve their validation skills.

Empathy and Assertiveness

One assertiveness training skill involves helping individuals to use both assertive requests and empathy to explain their point. For example, a person requests something of their partner kindly. "Would you please wait to feed the cat until after I leave? The smell of the food disgusts me," says Jason. His girlfriend Jenna responds, "That's not how I usually do my routine. I have a certain way I like to do things." Jason first expresses empathy and then asserts his request kindly again. "I get that you have a typical routine and it could be difficult to change something you are used to. It would mean a lot to me though if you were willing to try to shift it for me. It's a small thing really." Jenna responds, "I don't understand why it is such a big deal. Can't you just get over it?" Jason expresses empathy and asserts himself again. "I could see why you felt I was making a big deal. It is not ultimately life threatening. It is just one small thing you could do that would make my life a little better. Would you please consider it?" Jenna thinks about it and states, "Yeah whatever. It isn't really a big deal. I'll feed the cat after you leave. But you owe me one," she jokes with a smile.

Clinicians can guide couples in using this skill with each other by having them pick a small disagreement to discuss. This skill typically works best for clients who struggle to be assertive. During the discussion, the clinician should guide each person in first showing empathy and then asking for their request or stating their opinion. For example, if a couple is discussing date nights, the discussion may go like this:

Person A: I would like to have more date nights.

Person B: We really don't have enough time for more date nights. We are strapped for time as it is.

Person A (using the skill): You are right. We have barely enough time to get anything done, let alone add more date nights. And, I need more time with you. I miss you.

Person B (using the skill): I understand that you miss me and want more "us" time. And, I need us to stop adding extra activities to our plates. All these extra things keep us from getting that extra alone time.

When clinicians notice a client not using the skill, they can gently guide their clients back toward using the skill. The skill can help clients practice using empathy while also stating their needs.

Forgiveness

Most clinicians and individuals will report that forgiveness is one of the most important factors in sustaining a long and happy marriage (Fincham, Paleari, and Regalia, 2002). Forgiveness is an empathy skill because it often requires an individual to find a way to understand why their partner did something that may have been hurtful. For example, to forgive someone for lying, an individual has to consider why their partner felt they needed to lie. In another example, if a couple had a big argument in which names were called, forgiveness might require an individual to consider their partner's state of mind before they can consider moving on. Maybe their partner felt trapped or hurt, and then they lashed out.

Forgiveness can be a helpful concept to discuss with pre-marital clients for a variety of reasons. For some clients, they have never really thought about the role forgiveness will play in their relationship. For other clients, they have never really learned how to forgive. Clinicians have an opportunity to teach clients how to forgive.

When teaching forgiveness to clients, I start an open dialogue with clients about what their forgiveness process involves. I encourage each person to share an example of how they needed to forgive someone in the past and what steps helped them to accomplish that forgiveness.

Common themes I hear from clients include: putting themselves in the other person's shoes; reminding themselves of all the positive qualities that person possesses; allowing time to pass; hearing an apology for a wrongdoing. There are no wrong answers for how individuals need to forgive, but each person can learn from their partner some valuable tools to forgive better.

Usually, I will write some of the client's steps on the white board. Discussing forgiveness can be a great way for couples to bring up unresolved issues they may still be dealing with in their relationship.

If clients find the discussion difficult, I explain some of the steps in my own forgiveness process. First, I have to make a conscious decision to forgive someone. Second, I have to find a way to understand why they did something that was hurtful. I usually try to come up with a more neutral or positive reframe for their action. I also try to consider ways I may have acted negatively if I were put in the same situation. Third, I decide whether the relationship is repairable or if I need to create a boundary to protect myself from further harm. If there is a boundary I need to set, I try to ask for my need directly from the person (if they are the kind of person who will listen and respect that boundary). Finally, I choose to consciously think of other things when the action comes up in my head and move on. Usually, doing this over time helps me forgive.

Empathy Thoughts

Geri, a mother of three and wife to James, had a terrible day. Her boss yelled at her for not fixing a mistake that no one informed her about. She worked through lunch and was in a very bad mood on her way home. As she drove, she began thinking about what she needed to get done that night. She thought about how nice it would be if James had made dinner. Then, she thought to herself, "he never makes dinner, why would he now? I bet he wouldn't even make dinner if I asked." She continued to ruminate angrily about how little help she gets from her husband. When she got home, no dinner was made and she sarcastically stated, "I guess you couldn't be considerate enough to make dinner for us." A huge argument ensued.

This is an example of how negative thinking can create negative outcomes in life. In Cognitive Behavioral Therapy this is called *mind reading*—assuming one knows what their partner is thinking without communicating (Nichols and Schwartz, 2006). If Geri had used some empathy thoughts prior to coming home, she might have had a better outcome. An empathy thought is simply replacing a negative thought with a more empathetic or neutral way of thinking about another person. For example, Geri might first have her negative thought about her partner, but then intentionally shift the thought to a more neutral or empathetic thought such as, "He might be just as busy as I am," or "he may have had a rough day today too." When Geri shifts her thoughts to a more empathetic one, she is more likely to approach her husband with a kinder approach and say, "Babe, would you mind cooking dinner for us tonight. I had a rough day."

A good time to use this skill is when the clinician notices a client or clients that commonly engage in very negative thought patterns or assumptions. Clinicians can teach this skill to clients by modeling the behavior in session and then explaining what they are doing to clients. For example, a clinician may state, "When you are thinking more positively about your partner, it tends to make it easier to respond to your partner." The clinician can then ask the couple for examples of ways they could use empathy thoughts day to day in their personal life.

Rookie Mistakes

When teaching forgiveness, clinicians may learn that some clients will not know what it takes to forgive or will recognize that they tend to hold grudges. In these cases, it is helpful to explore why an individual client struggles to forgive. I often will ask about how their families handled difficulties and what they learned about forgiveness from parents. Finally, I explore whether there are differences between the kinds of actions that warrant forgiveness. For example, some people can forgive smaller mistakes but really struggle with big mistakes such as affairs or lies. Through this exploration, I can often help clients to begin to develop a way to practice forgiving.

Another potential issue clinicians may face is that clients sometimes see empathy as giving in or caving in. In these circumstances, I try to reframe the way they think about empathy. An example I use is that when people feel heard, they are more willing to listen to your opinion. Empathy is a conscious way of opening your partner up to new ideas. I also try to give examples for how someone can be empathetic but still hold their own opinion.

One final potential issue clinicians may face is that clients will practice the skill for a time but then go back to old ways. In developing any skill, it is important to remember that research suggests it takes anywhere from 18 to 254 days to create a new habit (Clear, 2014).

Empathy is a habit like any other habit and requires conscious effort. During sessions, I model empathy and I even encourage clients to try to be empathetic or validating when we discuss the various other issues listed in this book. Reminding clients to use the skill during the sessions is one small way to reinforce the skill.

Practice Ideas

1. Explore two or more models of therapy. Look for themes related to empathy. Find and experiment with those interventions that clinicians use in the different models. See what fits for you.
2. Practice using the levels of validation in a supervision group with other clinicians. Have your fellow clinicians give you feedback for how you could improve these skills.
3. Do some deeper research on how different religions or groups teach forgiveness. What could you pull from the different groups that might be helpful to teach to your clients?

Bibliography

Angera, J.J. and Long, E.C.J. (2006). Qualitative and quantitative evaluations of an empathy training program for couples in marriage and romantic relationships. *Journal of Couple and Relationship Therapy*, 5(1), 1–26.

Carnelly, K.B., Maio, G.R., Thomas, G., and Fincham, F.D. (2008). Unraveling the role of forgiveness in family relationships. *Journal of Personality and Social Psychology*, 94(2), 307–319.

Clear, J. (2014). How long does it actually take to form a new habit? (Backed by Science). *Huffington Post*, June 10, www.huffingtonpost.com/james-clear/forming-new-habits_b_5104807.html.

Farrelly, P. and Farrelly, B. (1994). *Dumb and Dumber*. New Line Cinema.

Fincham, F.D., Paleari, G., and Regalia, C. (2002). Forgiveness in marriage: The role of relationship quality, attributions, and empathy. *Personal Relationships*, 9, 27–37.

Gottman, J.M., Coan, J., Carrerre, S., and Swanson, C. (1998). Predicting marital happiness and stability from newlywed interactions. *Journal of Marriage and the Family*, 60, 5–22.

Hall, K. (2015). Using the 6 levels of validation to improve the quality of your relationship. *Black Love and Marriage*, www.blackloveandmarriage.com/2013/04/using-the-6-levels-of-validation-to-improve-the-quality-of-your-relationships.

Headley, J. (2013). It's not about the Nail. *YouTube*, 22 May.

Linehan, M.M. (2015). *DBT Skills Training Manual*, 2nd ed. New York: The Guilford Press.

Long, E.C.J., Angera, J.J., Carter, S.J., Nakamoto, M., and Kalso, M. (1999). Understanding the one you love: A longitudinal assessment of an empathy training program for couples in romantic relationships. *Family Relations, 59*, 235–242.

Nichols, M.P. and Schwartz, R.C. (2006) *Family Therapy: Concepts and Methods*. Boston, MA: Pearson Education.

Seppola, E., Rossomando, T., and Doty, J.R. (2013). Social connection and compassion: Important predictors of health and well-being. *Social Research, 8*(2), 411–430.

Session Four

FIGHTING RESPECTFULLY

We both said, "I do!" and we haven't agreed on a single thing since.
Mike Myers, *So I Married an Axe Murderer*

Gina and Ben are a middle-aged couple I saw in counseling. They reported when things were good in their relationship, they were very good. However, when they fought, things got very bad. Gina often felt like Ben's enemy when they fought. He felt the same about her. Both were very stubborn and fought to win. Both would go to extreme measures to prove they were right such as name calling, yelling, and even throwing things at one another. At the end their fights, both felt like losers. The damage was often very hard to repair.

Fighting respectfully is the third habit for successful marriages. In the example above, Gina and Ben struggle to disagree in a respectful way. Not all couples' disagreements will involve such drastic circumstances, but there are still many ways that couples can fight disrespectfully. While we cannot expect couples to avoid arguments altogether, it is important to guide couples to disagree in ways that are less damaging to their relationship. In her article about what leads to divorce, Brigid Duffield (2013) states, "those of us who practice in family law see clients' lack of conflict-resolution skills and the resulting destruction of the marriage that drive couples to divorce" (p. 208). The way couples disagree has a huge impact on the way they view the health of their relationship. This is why it is so important to teach pre-marital couples healthy skills for conflict in the beginning of the relationship.

Fighting respectfully takes some work for both parties. Each individual must learn to manage their own emotions, to develop tools for ending an argument if things are getting too heated, and to find a way to negotiate for the best possible outcome for both parties. Beyond this, couples need to find a way to improve the way they interact going forward. In the case of Gina and Ben, one of the biggest lessons they had to learn was how to fight on the same team. Rather than fighting to prove the other person wrong, they needed to learn how to resolve conflict in a way that made both of them happy in the end. In this chapter, we will discuss some valuable tools that you can teach pre-marital couples to use to resolve conflict as a team.

Myths about Conflict

Through the years of counseling and couples therapy, most treatment models focused on teaching couples different ways to resolve conflict. It was believed that if the therapist could reduce the amount of conflict in the couple relationship, then the couple was in a better place and no longer in need of therapy.

In general, couples do not like to be in conflict. Conflict causes high levels of emotion, hurt feelings, and a general discomfort. Due to this response, there are some myths that exist regarding conflict. These myths exist in both the therapeutic world and in the world of our clients. In this chapter, we will explore some of these myths and how they may affect a couple's overall happiness.

Myth #1: Couples should be able to resolve all conflicts.

Reality: In his book *Why Marriages Succeed or Fail*, John Gottman (1995) discussed how many conflicts are not resolvable either due to personality or value differences. There is in fact no win/win solution available given the circumstance. These conflicts are instead managed. Gottman suggests that 50 percent of conflicts in marriage are in fact unsolvable.

For example, Tim and Jill disagree about the use of marijuana. Tim states that he wants to smoke marijuana because it helps him sleep at night and keeps his moods more calm. Jill, on the other hand, hates marijuana and wishes he never would bring it into their home.

She worries about his use and the impact it will have on their children if they find out he uses it. In this situation, neither party was willing to budge their opinion or willing to ultimately change their preference. In order to help them manage the situation better, I suggested Jill come up with ways that Tim could reduce the impact on her if he did smoke marijuana. Jill agreed that she could turn a blind eye to his use if he would smoke it at a friend's house and never let the children see him smoke. Since Tim mostly liked to smoke socially, he agreed that he would go over to his friend's house to smoke and walk home to be safe.

In this scenario, Jill and Tim never really came up with a win/win scenario. Both Tim and Jill will forever disagree about whether marijuana use is acceptable or not acceptable. However, each partner was able to shift their behavior enough to put the issue to rest. In this case, marijuana usage is managed, but not necessarily resolved. In many issues in couple's lives, they will not find an ultimate win/win solution to their conflict.

Myth #2: The absence of conflict means the relationship is healthy.

Reality: Conflict is a necessary evil in most relationships. While there are couples who rarely disagree, it is more common that they do have some conflict but they are likely trying to avoid bringing up the conflict. "Conflict can have a positive effect in our social life. It helps us resolve tension, and might promote unity between parties with intrinsic differences" (Meza-de-Luna and Romero-Zepeda, 2013, p. 87). Couples who can disagree, but still find a way to work out their differences tend to be happy. It is not conflict itself that causes harm in a relationship, but conflict that is not resolved in a respectful way, or not managed well.

There are situations in which a couple avoids conflict, but these situations are not always going perfectly. Gottman (1995) coined the term "conflict avoiders" to describe couples who tend to avoid conflict for the sake of keeping the peace in the relationship. I tend to see two types of conflict avoiders in counseling: 1) people who avoid conflict to the point of never or rarely getting their needs met with one another; and 2) people who avoid conflict up to a certain degree, but then have huge, life-shattering fights about once in a blue moon that bring up every conflict that has been avoided up until that point. In these cases, conflict avoiding is often a negative situation.

For example, Wanda and Michael had been married for 30 years. Both reported they got along quite well. When one partner was bothered, the other person would try to withdraw and give them space. They were in therapy because their sex life had become non-existent. They were so polite and kind that any slight sign of disinterest in sex caused the other one to respectfully retreat and give them space. When long periods of time passed, they funneled their energy into other activities—again to avoid putting any stress on their partner.

Over time, this led them to a sexless marriage. From the outside view, most people looked at their marriage as an ideal one because they never argued and had little to no conflict at all. Inside the marriage, both were very disappointed by the lack of sex and both were equally trying to be respectful of their partner's space. In this situation, they needed to learn to bring up this conflict a little more often so they could enjoy a more active sex life.

Myth #3: In a fight, there must be one winner and one loser.

Reality: Actually, fighting in this manner often causes serious resentments for the couples I work with in therapy. With one winner and one loser, you often find couples who are fighting to prove each other wrong. The issue with this type of fighting is couples can't find ways to either agree to disagree or move on from an issue they won't see eye to eye on.

To think about this concept in a different way, I often suggest to couples that fighting to win makes you both feel like losers. Yes, one person may win but they will win at the expense of their partner. That partner will then be very hurt and often for a long period of time afterwards. If one person loses you both lose.

The crazy thing about this type of fighting is that it usually involves a matter of preference. For example, Jerry and Elaine were fighting about how they should clean a coffee stain from the carpet. Jerry believed you should look up on the internet how to clean it and pick one of the methods listed. Elaine had previously cleaned a stain using dish detergent and water that had worked well, and wanted to use this before the coffee stain stuck to the carpet. The situation was dire, since coffee had just been spilled. In this example, both parties were offering different preferences for how they thought the stain should be cleaned. One could argue for either point of view, but the reality is that there is no exact right or wrong answer here, but merely a preference for how to handle a situation.

It is better to teach couples how to fight for win/win solutions or compromises in which they each give a little and take a little. It is also better to teach couples that there is a difference between having a different viewpoint versus believing what they think is a fact. Many individuals mistakenly have the belief that the way they do things is in fact the right way, when in reality it is often how they were taught to do things. There is no right or wrong in many social situations and there are many different solutions to problems.

Myth #4: Couples should resolve conflicts as soon as possible.

Reality: In many cases, it is a good idea for a couple to resolve a conflict right away so resentment does not fester. However, there are certain conflicts that are not going to be resolved in one sitting. Sometimes, this hard rule makes couples fight terribly and do things to each other they really can't take back. There are other situations that make it difficult to resolve a conflict right away, such as being in front of family members or friends. A couple that fights in front of others risks the chance of triangulating others into the fight.

Moss and Sean were raised in the Christian tradition and were always taught to never let the sun go down on their anger. When it came to arguments about their son with attention deficit disorder (ADD), they never seemed to agree about what to do in different situations. Moss was raised with spankings as a form of punishment and wanted to use this method in his teaching process with their son. Sean was raised this way as well, but when their son was diagnosed with ADD, he began to read different books on ADD that suggested other methods. They often argued for hours into the night about their differences of opinion.

They recognized that in the later hours they were not on their best behavior and the fights could get pretty bad.

In situations where disagreements may take a long time, it is in fact better for the couple to take breaks and sometimes talk about the issue over several days or even weeks to get to a mutually agreeable end. There is a point in arguments where the couple is out of control and saying things that they cannot take back. As in the example with Moss and Sean, they needed to have several short discussions about different parenting scenarios over several days or even weeks. Rather than continuing to discuss things in a disrespectful fashion, it is better for the couple to take frequent time outs if necessary.

Myth #5: Couples don't need to argue about every single issue.

Reality: It depends. The old advice given was you need to pick and choose your battles. Some issues need to be ignored or avoided while other issues need to be addressed. Couples need to find a way to discuss issues and get over them quickly. They also need to come up with a method for how to pick and choose their battles.

Darlene and Wayne were having difficulty with this belief. Darlene hated conflict so she always tried to avoid bringing issues up with her partner. Wayne would bring up issues and it would make Darlene mad because she wished he would "pick and choose" his battles—meaning she wished he didn't bring things up at all. However, she would often hold onto these conflicts and then have a bigger fight with Wayne later when he brought up issues with her.

I encourage my clients to develop a strategy together for how they will pick and choose their battles. For example, Darlene suggested that if one person repeatedly does a behavior, it should be addressed. If it was a one-time event, she asked Wayne to forgive her of the issue and not bring it up. In response, Wayne asked Darlene to bring her concerns up more often when she wasn't as bothered by the issue. This way, she could address her conflict with him in a nicer way. In this situation, it is clear that each party needed to try a different approach to their conflict. Sometimes a good outcome is to encourage a couple to address conflict more often.

How to Teach Clients to Fight Respectfully

When working with pre-marital clients, it is always helpful to discuss different ways they can address conflict more effectively. In the following sections, we will go over a variety of ways you can guide your clients to address conflict in kinder, more respectful ways. There is no one perfect means for getting through conflict. However, these skills discuss ways couples can manage their issues more effectively.

Effective Time Outs

In the 2014 popular television show *How I Met your Mother* (Fryman, 2014), Lily and Marshall, a married couple in the show, have not seen each other in weeks due to a trip Marshall took away to visit his family. During his time away, he is offered a position as a judge, his lifelong dream. He accepts the position without discussing it with his wife Lily. When Marshall comes back into town, he knows he and his wife will have a fight about this decision. However, when he gets there, they both use the phrase "pause" to put the fight on hold and spend some quality time with each other first. This was a perfect example of how a couple can use a time out in their favor. In a couple's life, there will be many times when they have fights that either get too big or are too challenging to resolve in one sitting. Rather than trying to resolve everything at once, sometimes it is better to put a disagreement on hold until a couple is ready to honestly tackle the issue as a team.

The "time out" is a helpful skill a couple can develop to prevent arguments from taking a bad turn or to stop an argument when it is getting to a point where they are hurting one another. "In some cases, it can be the only thing that keeps a verbal dispute from turning physical" (Brenoff, 2012, p. 1). When explaining the reason to use time outs to couples, I often explain that time out is a way of saying, "I love you more than I love this argument."

You can guide your clients to use the time out by asking them to personally identify when they think it would be best to call a time out. Scaling questions from solution-focused therapy (Nichols and Schwartz, 2005) can be used to help individuals develop awareness of their personal anger levels. For example, a clinician may ask, "If you were to think of your anger as a scale of 1–10 with one being lightly irritated and ten being completely out of control, at what number do you think you should take a time out?" You may also ask them to describe what their anger looks like at the different numbers, "What does a 6 look like? What's the difference between a 6 and a 10 for you?" I generally suggest couples try to stay at a 5 or 6 or below on the anger scale when they are discussing a conflict.

Once they have established when to take a time out, clinicians can teach clients how to take an effective time out. Couples must use four important steps:

1.   Use a word or phrase that both parties have agreed to use.
2.   Go into separate spaces for an agreed upon period of time.
3.   Use that time to calm down.
4.   Come back when you are ready to listen to your partner and discuss the disagreement more respectfully.

In step 1, therapists can have couples identify a word or phrase that has meaning to them. Time out phrases are most effective when couples agree to what is said and agree to the meaning behind the phrase. For example, one couple I worked with used the phrase "Bruce!" to call a time out. Bruce was a friend of theirs that sometimes would say things that were very awkward. Calling that name out loud was an inside joke that helped them to laugh in the moment and take a step back. After hearing the word Bruce, they both understood they were taking a time out until things calmed down. Other phrases can be "Pause," "I need a time out," or couples can also use agreed upon hand gestures if they prefer.

After establishing the phrase, clinicians can help the client decide when and where to take the time out. I typically suggest couples only use 30 minutes to 2 hours as a time out, with some flexibility if the argument starts at an inconvenient time. For example, if an argument started right before bed, it is okay to sleep on it and discuss the issue in the morning. As another example, if after 2 hours one partner is still not calm they can opt to lengthen the time out for another hour. The couple also should decide where a time out takes place. For example, some couples have separate rooms while others agree to let one person go for a walk or a drive while the other person stays at the house.

During the time out, individuals need to calm down. Every person is different in what things actually calm them down. This can be a great potential area for clinicians to explore. You might ask, "What helps you personally to calm down when you are angry?" Some examples of ways people calm down include deep breathing, playing video games, taking a bath, going for a walk or exercising, doing chores, etc. Have your clients come up with one or two plans for how they will personally calm down.

After calming down, the individual has two important tasks: putting their thoughts or hurts into clearer words and getting ready to listen to their partner's perspective. First, the individual needs to get a clearer picture of what is bothering them and put those thoughts into words.

Clinicians can guide clients to put their feelings into actionable needs or wants. For example, "I was hurt when you forgot to pick up our son," can be reframed into an actionable need, "In the future, can we talk on the phone early in the day so we can plan ahead for scheduling pickups?"

The second task is for the individual to get themselves ready to listen to a different perspective. While one person may come up with a few good solutions, there are still two people in the discussion. It is important for each individual to be ready to listen to and really respect their partner's perspective on the issue before going back into the discussion.

Finally, the couple must come back and discuss the topic. The only way for a time out to be most effective is if both parties make a conscious effort to come back and resolve it together peacefully.

Negotiation and Compromise

In marriage, there will be many differences of opinion which will require some negotiation. In pre-marital counseling, it can be a good idea to teach clients about the different negotiation styles and teach them when to use each style of negotiation. The five negotiating styles are competing, accommodating, avoiding, collaborating, and compromising (Coburn, 2015).

You are at a car dealership. The dealer is asking for $25,000. You've done your research and you know it is worth $23,000. You make him an offer of $22,000. He goes back into the office and talks to some imaginary boss who is going to refuse. He comes back with an offer of $24,000. You know better and you tell him it's $22,000 or you're going to walk. He hesitates. You hit the pavement. Just as you walk out that door, the dealer grabs you and says he'll make your $22,000 work. You win!

This is an example of a competing negotiation style. Each person does whatever they can to take care of themselves and the expression, "My way or the highway!" is commonly used to describe people who use this style. Buying a car is a perfect example of when to use this negotiation style. However, in marriage, it is not usually the best style of negotiation to use.

The accommodating style of negotiation is one in which the individual neglects their own needs in order to accommodate those around them (Furgerson, 2015). These people typically will give their right arm to make sure those around them are happy. However, they tend to take on too much and are sometimes described as "Martyrs." This style may work if you are married to another accommodating negotiator or with a collaborator. However, there will be some clear roadblocks if this type of negotiator is marrying a competing negotiator.

The avoiding style is one in which people are still going to do things their way, but they won't discuss it with their partner. Instead they try to avoid the issue altogether (Furgerson, 2015). For example, I had a client whose wife asked him not to take his former mistress secretary to lunch for Secretary's Day. Rather than being direct or negotiating for something different, he stopped the conversation, led her to believe he would follow through with her request, and later took the secretary out for lunch.

The collaborating style of negotiation is when one person will consider both perspectives and try to come up with win/win solutions. "Collaborative negotiators are willing to invest more time and energy in finding innovative solutions" (Coburn, 2015, p. 4). A win/win solution is one in which both partners leave the situation happy with the outcome (Covey, 2005). The partner will try to listen clearly, hear where they are coming from, and often think outside of the box in order to find win/win solutions. They feel their needs are just as important as the needs of those around them.

Finally, the compromising negotiation style is one in which each party gets a little bit of what they want and sacrifices some of the things they want. I refer to these as half-wins. For example, Jeanie and Michael received $1000 tax return. Jeanie wanted to spend the money on finishing the basement. Michael wanted to fence in the yard. Ultimately there is a finite amount of money to spend. A compromise or half-win is for Jeanie and Michael to split the money 50/50. Each of them gets $500 and gets to choose how they will use the money for their house.

Not every negotiation style is going to work when you are in a relationship. The competing style shown in our example of negotiation has its place in the work environment or a sales environment. It works because most people can put their feelings aside and stick to business. You really don't care much about how the other person feels afterwards. The ultimate goal is to get what you want and get the most out of the situation for yourself. For people who can negotiate with no feelings involved and stick to business, this style is perfect.

In a relationship, you do care about your partner. Negotiation styles that are cutthroat and don't consider the other person really do not have a place in a relationship where a couple chooses to fight respectfully. Ideally, couples should work toward using collaborative styles of negotiation. In some cases, the accommodating negotiation style or the compromising style can also be helpful for couples. The one exception is if you have one partner who is very extreme about their opinions. "People that take the most extreme positions tend to get more of what is on offer" (Coburn, 2015, p. 3). For these individuals, even if they are compromising, they will likely get more of what they personally desire than their partner who may take a less extreme approach.

Clinicians can teach these different styles by doing the following steps:

1. Present the five negotiation styles to your clients and describe them in detail.

2. Ask which style they tend to use the most.
3. Ask your clients to identify the pros and cons they have seen in their own life when using their style or other negotiation styles.
4. Have the couple practice using the negotiation styles that they prefer in session.
5. Ask the couple to identify one to two steps they could personally take to work toward becoming better negotiators with one another.

Apologies

I see a lot of couples make the mistake of avoiding apologies or giving ineffective apologies. This is a problem because without an apology, arguments can last for a very long time.

The most effective apologies have four steps:

1. Say out loud, "I am sorry . . ."
2. Take ownership for something you did wrong.
3. Offer a repair or a way to resolve the situation going forward.
4. Reconnect (Gottman, 1995).

Stating the apology out loud is very important. I have heard clients state that an apology is implied in some cases, but I can't stress enough how important it can be to truly hear the words. For Jim and Karen, stating an apology out loud carried a lot of weight. Karen stated in session, "He never apologizes for anything he does!" Jim was very confused by her statement. He replied, "I always try to apologize. I cook for you. I get you flowers. I try to be nicer to you. How is that not an apology?"

In this example, Jim was trying to be apologetic by showing his wife he was sorry. Since he had never said the words out loud, Karen had assumed he wasn't apologetic at all. She believed he was just doing those things to avoid the issue. Over time, Karen had developed resentment that Jim had never acknowledged he had done something to hurt her. She saw his apologetic actions as a means to try and kiss up to her, rather than a way to apologize.

Step 2 of an effective apology is to take ownership. There is a difference between taking ownership and making excuses. When someone makes excuses, they put the responsibility everywhere else. They blame other people, work, or other priorities. When a person takes ownership, they place the full responsibility on themselves. For example, Karen states, "I am sorry I yelled at you, but you know bringing up my mother makes me angry!" This is an example of making an excuse. While she apologized for her action, she blamed it on Jim's choice to bring up her mother. If Karen was taking ownership, she would say, "I am sorry I yelled at you. I was angry, but anger does not give me an excuse to yell. I don't want to hurt you." In this example, Karen puts the full responsibility for her actions on herself.

Step 3 of an effective apology is to find a way to repair the situation. Someway, somehow, find a way to fix the situation going forward so it won't happen again. Pick repairs that can either be done in the present or in the very near future. Follow through with any repair given. In the situation with Karen and Jim, Karen could offer a repair for yelling such as, "I will keep my voice calm for the rest of the discussion," or if the argument is over she could say, "I will try to keep my voice calm in future discussions."

Sometimes your clients will not know the best way to repair. In these cases, you can guide your clients to ask their partner for suggestions. In the case of Karen and Jim, they can be encouraged to say, "What can I do to make things right? I just want to make you happy and I don't know how." This question still gives the intent that they want to help; they are just not sure what the next step should be.

Step 4 of an effective apology is to reconnect. Clinicians can help couples to identify what helps them feel closer after an argument. Some couples prefer to hug or kiss. Other couples try to spend some fun time together. There are couples who will state things they appreciate about one another to intentionally change the mood. In the case with Jim and Karen, Jim's attempts to cook for his wife or buy flowers could be seen as attempts to reconnect. His efforts would be more fruitful after he did the first three steps of the apology. Either way, help your clients to find a way to reconnect that works best for them.

This can help couples move on more quickly from an argument. A good apology helps a couple restore their intimacy and sometimes helps them feel closer at the end of an argument (Markman, Stanley, and Blumberg, 2010).

Fighting No-nos!

When you are guiding couples through the habit of fighting respectfully, it is important to assess for and address fighting habits that will cause harm in a relationship. The following section discusses various problematic behaviors your couples may engage in during their arguments. In this final section, I will address how you can encourage change in these areas with your clients.

Interpersonal Violence

Violence of any kind should be avoided. If you detect that a couple may be immersed in violence in their arguments, it is important to address it quickly. In some cases, it can be helpful to split the couple apart during sessions to get a clear picture as to how bad the violence has gotten. If at any time you feel the couple is in serious harm, please don't hesitate to refer clients to domestic violence shelters, children's division, or any other domestic violence resources you have in your community. Also, remember you are a mandatory reporter. If at any time you detect that a child has witnessed or been a part of a domestic violence situation, it is your obligation as a clinician to report that infraction to your local child abuse department.

In this section, we are looking more specifically at intimate partner violence. There are cases in your sessions when you will work with a couple that is getting violent during their arguments. This is considered intimate partner violence. "Intimate partner violence includes acts of physical aggression, psychological abuse, forced intercourse and other forms of sexual coercion, and various controlling behaviors such as isolating a person from family and friends or restricting access to information and assistance" (World Health Organization, 2002, p. 1).

Sometimes, you will see a couple engaged in intimate partner violence. Your instinct as a therapist may be to suggest they terminate the relationship. It is okay to state your concern to your clients about their safety, but to also respect that they will likely make their own decision regarding whether to stay or leave the relationship.

In some cases, a potential intervention for clinicians can be to help the couple create a safety contract that includes specific steps each person will take to prevent the argument from getting out of control. Steps a couple can take may include asking for a time out, going to a friend's or family member's home, and calling the police. The contract can also discuss when and where certain discussions should happen. For example, if parenting is a typical discussion that ends in violence, the couple may agree to only have those conversations in a public place or with the therapist until they get to a point of more control.

Clinicians should assess for potential mental illness or substance abuse in violent partners. If these factors are present, clinicians should refer clients for additional treatment such as anger management, psychiatric treatment with medication management for mental illnesses, and substance abuse treatment.

Below the Belt Comments

In a relationship, couples learn deep and vulnerable secrets about each other. However, couples are notorious for bringing up these vulnerabilities in arguments. I call these comments "Below the Belt" because these comments are unfair, underhanded tactics (Martin, 2015). For example, John had expressed to Susie that when he was growing up, people called him stupid all the time. He sometimes feels stupid today when he tries to explain his point of view because he never really learned how to communicate his thoughts well. Susie knows this is a sore spot for John. Sometimes during arguments, Susie calls him "stupid". In this case, "stupid" is a below the belt comment because it is a known insecurity that Susie is using against John in the argument.

One intervention is to have each individual list the specific comments they personally consider below the belt comments prior to their session.

In session, the couple can discuss why these statements or words are so triggering. Once each person knows these hot buttons, the therapist can encourage each individual to avoid using these words or phrases.

Fighting in Front of Others

Jamie and Ashton clearly had a fight before they came to dinner with their friends. They both have angry faces. They are short with each other and they are short with those around them. They say slightly off-kilter comments to each other throughout dinner. They are trying to have a good time, but it is clear to those around them that things are not going well. There are many situations in which a couple is in front of others but disagreeing. Couples may find themselves in front of kids, relatives, friends, and even business associates.

In situations like these, there are a couple of strategies clinicians can offer to help clients navigate their arguments. First, help your couple develop a way to reassure each other non-verbally. This can include a loving touch of the shoulder, a firm touch to the leg, or a facial expression of kindness. It is important that the clinician establish with the couple what this gesture means. An example of what the gesture can mean: "I know we can't discuss this right now, but we will. I still love you and want to have a good time." Another example of what the touch can mean is, "I didn't mean to hurt you just then. I am sorry." Regardless of the meaning, make sure the couple agrees to what they think the gesture will mean going forward.

Helping couples to develop their own non-verbal language prevents some arguments from getting worse. In a situation where one person offended the other person, the quick, reassuring touch can let them know they are apologetic and want to make things right.

In some situations, couples need to know when to step away and discuss things on their own. Clinicians can guide couples to take little time outs and go to the bathroom or their car. If the argument was big enough that they cannot enjoy the situation, it's better to cancel the plans or show up late if need be so they can resolve their issues peacefully.

Rookie Mistakes

One potential problem you may see in your couples is the overusage of apologies. For example, some clients have learned that an apology can end an argument and they use it basically to get their partner to stop talking. An apology is only effective if it is given after developing a clear understanding of what is hurting the other partner. This requires each individual to actually listen to their partner. Clinicians should guide clients to slow down, hear their partner, and then apologize.

When negotiating, another potential mistake couples may experience is something I like to call "negotiating before coming to the table." Since partners know each other very well, they often begin considering their partner's perspective before asking for what they want. Then, instead of asking for what they originally wanted, they compromise and suggest their compromised idea to their partner. When their partner hears their idea, they are ready to negotiate for their own interests. Since the original partner already compromised in their head, they get angry when met with resistance.

For example, Meredith wants to go to Taco Bell. She knows that sometimes William doesn't like Taco Bell. Rather than asking to go to Taco Bell, Meredith negotiates or compromises in her head. When she states what she wants out loud to William, she asks to go to Hardees. William is not really in the mood for Hardees and suggests Wendy's. Meredith then gets upset because she already compromised on her original want in her head before asking. She fights tooth and nail to go to Hardees. William is then either confused or angered by her unwillingness to compromise.

William is negotiating at the table. He heard her request, and assumed the request was negotiable. He negotiated out loud with his partner. Meredith negotiated before coming to the table. She had already compromised in her head, which made her less willing to compromise again out loud.

Clinicians can challenge clients to consider their original want by asking for them to identify an ideal situation. Most people won't get everything they want when they negotiate. One of the best strategies for effective negotiation is to aim high! If you notice your clients doing this, you can encourage them to first identify what they ideally want before looking at the situation practically.

Practice Ideas

1. Do some of your own research on negotiation styles. Take some courses about how to become a better negotiator.
2. Practice using time outs in your own sessions when couples are getting out of hand. Clinicians can model healthy conflict by guiding couples to take time outs when appropriate. This can be extremely helpful when a session seems to be getting out of control.
3. Take any Gottman training courses or read any of his books. Gottman has written several helpful books on how to manage couple conflict. If you are interested, he offers certification.

Bibliography

Brenoff, A. (2012). Time-Out Signals: What's your marriage problem solver? *Huffington Post*, www.huffingtonpost.com/2012/02/22/time-out-signals-marriage-problem-solvers_n_1279820.html.

Coburn, C. (2015). *Negotiation Conflict Styles*. The Negotiation Training Experts, Ombuds Office, http://hms.harvard.edu/sites/default/files/assets/Sites/Ombuds/files/NegotiationConflictStyles.pdf.

Covey, S.R. (2005). *The Seven Habits of Highly Effective People*. New York: DC Books.

Duffield, B. (2013). Reasons why conflict in marriage can deter divorce, *American Journal of Family Law, 27*(3), 208–211.

Fryman, P. (2014). *Unpause. How I Met your Mother, 9*, 15. Bays Thomas Productions.

Furgerson, J. (2015). *Five Negotiation Styles for Managing Conflict*. EHow. Demand Media, www.ehow.com/list_6569615_five-negotiation-styles-managing-conflict.html.

Gottman, J. (1995). *Why Marriages Succeed or Fail*. New York: Simon & Schuster.

Markman, H.J., Stanley, S.M., and Blumberg, S.L. (2010). *Fighting for Your Marriage: A Deluxe Revised Edition for Enhancing Marriage and Preventing Divorce*. San Francisco, CA: Jossey-Bass.

Martin, G. (2015). The meaning and origin of the expression: Below the belt. Phrase finder, www.phrases.org.uk/meanings/61100.html.

Meza-de-Luna, M.E. and Romero-Zepeda, H. (2013). Areas of conflict in the intimate couple, *Trames, 17*(67/62, 1), 87–100.

Nichols, M.P. and Schwartz, R.C. (2005). *Family Therapy: Concepts and Methods*, 7th ed. New York: Allyn & Bacon.

Schlamme, T. (1993). *So I Married an Axe Murderer*. TriStar Pictures.

World Health Organization (2002). *Intimate Partner Violence*, www.who.int/violence_injury_prevention/violence/world_report/factsheets/en/ipvfacts.pdf.

Session Five

ASKING FOR NEEDS AND WANTS EFFECTIVELY

Marriages don't work when one partner is happy and the other is miserable.
Marriage is about both people being equally miserable.

Joe Mantegna, *Forget Paris*

Kenneth and Julie were the proud parents of two beautiful children. They had been married for five years and suddenly were having trouble in their marriage. They found themselves fighting more about little things that never were a problem prior to children. Julie stated, "I have changed now that I am a mother. I need more from him than I ever have before." Kenneth felt baffled by this because he felt he was still the same person. He recognized that he could be a hard person to live with and that he got mad about stupid things at times. Why all of a sudden was he not a good enough partner for his wife?

The fourth habit that is vital for a healthy relationship is for each individual to identify their personal needs and desires so they can effectively communicate this information to their partner. In the above example, the needs in the relationship had changed. Prior to kids, Kenneth was likely meeting Julie's needs in small random acts of kindness here and there. However, once Julie had kids, she was constantly needed by the children. After further exploration, Julie recognized that she needed more kindness from Kenneth to feel supported in her role as a parent.

Needs and wants in a relationship can be complex because they change over time. Each individual in a relationship has different needs and wants but it is not always clear who is responsible for meeting those needs and wants. The happiest couples find a healthy balance between meeting their own needs and meeting the needs of their partner.

However, this habit takes some work. Individuals need to be able to do the following:

1. Clearly identify your personal need or want in the situation.
2. Decide whether you should meet this need/want by yourself or if you could use help from your partner.
3. If a partner is required, communicate the need/want to your partner in a respectful way.
4. In response, your partner chooses to meet the needs, negotiates for a compromise, or makes it easier for you to meet the need yourself.

If both individuals in a couple learn to use this process, couples can feel as though their needs and wants are respected and taken care of in their relationship.

Myths about Relationship Needs and Wants

If we were to look back at marriages long ago, we would see a much different picture of marriage than we do today. Marriage initially was a contract that created a family. People married for political, social, or economic gain and considered themselves lucky if they also got along well with their partner. Early marriage was seen as a way of making alliances and a means to get more help around the home (Ghose, 2013). Most people understood that marriage would meet the basic needs for food, shelter, clothing, and financial stability.

In marriages today, people expect a lot more from their partners—love, affection, friendship, emotional support, parental support, financial stability, a good sex life, and ultimate happiness. Is that too much to ask? These high expectations can put a lot of pressure on individuals. While it is ideal to meet each other's needs and wants, there are some myths about whose responsibility it is to meet needs and wants. There are also some myths about how possible it is to have every need met by your partner.

Myth #1: When you have been in a relationship for a while, you should be able to intuitively recognize your partner's needs.

Reality: While there will be some things you can recognize, needs and wants change over time. Many couples I work with talk about how their partner assumes they know what is wanted in a situation. When challenged to state that assumption out loud to their partner, it is not always accurate.

Terrence and Belinda were a couple fighting about wrong assumptions. Belinda asked, "Did you wear your ring today?" He replied, "Of, course I wore my ring today." His voice took on a higher inflection, and his wife assumed that he was being defensive. When he tried to correct her and say, "No, I wasn't being defensive. Sometimes I just get expressive with my voice, but she assumes that I am angry." Even though he tried to explain that his excitement sometimes may sound like anger, she could not change her assumption that he was angry.

In cognitive behavioral couples therapy, assumptions are described as "what each believes people and relationships are actually like" (Gurman, 2008, p. 52). It is common to make connections or predictions about a person's behavior. However, making assumptions can prevent individuals from giving their partner the benefit of the doubt. While in some cases, Terrence might have been angry, he is not angry every time his voice gets expressive. Instead of expecting to intuitively know a partner's needs or wants, it is better to ask and find out what these needs actually are. There are times when a person can be wrong.

Myth #2: It is not my partner's job to meet my needs. I should be able to take care of myself.

Reality: This is an extreme statement for a relationship. Relationships by their very nature exist to create a system in which couples can rely on each other to varying degrees. While it is important to meet some of your own needs, there should be a balance of meeting the needs of the self versus asking a partner for help.

Some individuals struggle to accept help from others because they have developed a dismissive or avoidant attachment style. In the healthiest relationships, individuals are securely attached which means the individual has a level of secure dependence on their partner. They are happy being both independent and dependent in their relationships.

"There is no such thing as complete independence from others or overdependence. There is only effective or ineffective dependence" (Johnson, 2004, p. 38).

Individuals who are dismissive or avoidant will do everything for everyone else, but rarely ask for or accept help from others. They struggle to accept help from others and they struggle to open up and be vulnerable. For example, Mary was in therapy because she and her life partner Jill were not having sex. Mary reported she was tired of taking care of everyone else. Jill struggled because many times in the past she tried to do things for Mary but to no avail. Mary would offer to do the dishes, but Jill would take this personally. Jill stated, "When I let her do the dishes, I felt guilty because I had not done them." To which Mary replied, "No, I wanted to help, but when I noticed it kept starting fights, I stopped doing the dishes. Then you kept complaining that you never got any help."

The challenge with this myth is that it puts the individual in a lose/lose situation. If you need help, this belief can keep you from asking for the help needed or accepting help when it is given. Instead, couples need to find the best possible balance of both giving and receiving in the relationship. In some cases, clinicians may need to guide an individual in learning to be more accepting of help from their partners.

Myth #3: My partner is responsible for meeting all of my emotional needs. If I am unhappy, it is a result of him/her not being a good partner.

Reality: This is also too extreme a statement. Just like in the previous example, one needs a balance between giving and taking from a relationship. Your partner can meet some of your needs. However, sometimes your partner is in a bad spot and has needs of their own. In these cases, you need to be responsible for meeting your own needs until your partner is in a better place to help out.

For example, there are times in a relationship when one partner is depressed. Common symptoms of depression include fatigue or loss of energy, psychomotor retardation or slowing down, and diminished interest or pleasure in all or most activities (American Psychiatric Association, 2013). When a partner is depressed, they have trouble meeting their own needs. An individual may find their partner in bed or lying on the couch throughout the day and avoiding activities. When dealing with a depressed partner, an individual often feels as though their needs don't matter. This is a situation in which the depressed person needs to focus on taking care of themselves. The partner also needs to focus on self-care while their depressed partner is taking action to improve their well-being.

While it is good to work on meeting each other's needs in a relationship, I think a better statement would be, "Take care of yourself so you can take care of those around you." Individuals who engage in regular self-care are often more capable of being available to meet the needs of a partner, family members, or friends.

Myth #4: Wants are not as important as needs in a relationship.

Reality: Wants over time become needs. As in everything in life, there should be some sort of balance. It is important to prioritize things in life and meet needs to the best of your ability. However, people still need to have joy. Joy comes from getting some of your wants or desires met as well.

For example, Bob and Denise came into therapy because they struggled with finances. "We have no money so we can't spend any-thing," Bob said. Denise eagerly agreed. However, their restrictive financial ideals prevented them from doing many fun things. They stopped going on dates or buying games. When they did have money, their way of having fun together was to go out to eat together and watch a movie. Now that money was scarce, they avoided everything enjoyable they used to do to connect. All conversations now focused on getting work done around the house or the problems they were going through.

Couples who struggle financially still have free time and need to find ways to connect and enjoy life. Rather than cutting everything out, sometimes the best option is to create a very small budget for such items so that every now and then, they can still have a fun evening out. In the case of Denise and Bob, I suggested they create free or very low-cost dates such as walking around a mall or taking a picnic to the park. This way, they still set aside time together for the fun things in life.

Pleasure and leisure are examples of wants or desires. While needs are important to take care of, wants are important components to having a quality of life.

Teaching Your Clients to Meet Needs and Wants Effectively

If you have been a clinician for a while, then you likely have noticed a common trend among our client populations—it is often difficult for them to identify their needs and clearly state these needs to the people around them. This is why it is imperative that we teach new couples to do this skill. So many people have not learned effective strategies for getting needs and wants met.

In pre-marital counseling, there are a few goals clinicians should focus on regarding needs and wants. The first goal is to help clients identify their emotional needs and wants. A need can be a small thing such as a partner listening to a story or a big thing such as a partner being there at the hospital during childbirth. The second goal is to help clients respectfully discuss needs and wants with one another. If clients aren't clear with each other about what they need, it can be difficult for a partner to do anything to help. The third goal is to help a partner really hear what their partner needs and find ways to spring into action. In this section, we will go over a few skills that can help you achieve these goals with your clients.

Identify Common Needs in Relationships

Sarah and Jason were in therapy to work on relationship issues. Sarah reported she didn't trust Jason because she could never count on him for things she needed. He stated he always tried to do things to make her happy. He would buy her flowers or get her some gifts when times were tough. Sarah stated that while those things were nice, he would not follow through on more important things such cleaning out the storage bin so they could get rid of it and have extra money around. Or financially, when they were strapped, he stated he would take over the bills, but often forgot to pay bills on time. This got them into more debt. Jason was good at taking care of her wants but not at taking care of her needs.

When working with pre-marital couples, it is important to teach them how to clearly identify and work toward meeting needs and wants. One skill I will use is to teach common needs people have in life. One easy method is to discuss Maslow's Hierarchy of Needs. Maslow's hierarchy describes the various needs people have in their lives. At the base of the pyramid are physiological needs such as food, water, sex, sleep, etc. Moving up, the next level is security and includes security of the body, of health, of the family, of employment, and of property. The level above includes love and belonging. The level above that includes self-esteem, and the top level includes actualization (Markel, 2014).

Each level needs to be taken care of before a person can focus on the next level. In the case of Sarah and Jason, above, Sarah's needs at level 2, "security" were not being met, which made it hard for her to recognize Jason's attempts to show love at level 3, "love and belonging."

As a clinician, you would use Maslow's pyramid to explain the importance of meeting the different needs at all levels. After explaining the different needs, you can have the couple discuss areas in their own relationship they could improve upon at every level. The types of questions you may ask to guide this activity include, "What needs aren't being met in your relationship?" "Who is responsible for meeting these needs?" "When should you meet your own needs rather than relying on your partner to meet the needs?" "How can you make a better effort to meet needs as a team?" Asking these questions can help your clients begin to look more closely at how to divide responsibility in the relationship.

Cognitive Restructuring

When a clinician notices that one or both individuals have a reactive or defensive attitude toward their partner, it can be helpful to explore internal thoughts/cognitions that may be contributing to the problem. When an individual has negative thought processes about their partner, arguments can become more intense. When exploring these internal thought processes, a clinician may decide to teach the individuals how to use cognitive restructuring to change the way they approach their partner.

Cognitive restructuring involves identifying common cognitive distortions and challenging those negative thinking patterns. Common distortions include: 1) dichotomous thinking such as all-or-nothing thinking; 2) catastrophic thinking or giving too much credit to the worst possible outcome; 3) labeling/mislabeling, which involves over generalizing a person's behavior as some type of character flaw (Evans, 2004).

To teach cognitive restructuring, first notice whether a client is using negative or self-defeating thoughts. If they are doing so, you can encourage them to begin to replace those thoughts with more neutral or positive thoughts when they recognize it. Finally, once they have replaced those thoughts, you can encourage them to either take some sort of positive action such as self-care or to seek help from their partner.

For example, Jenny tends to get a lot of validation from her partner Tom. However, there are some days when Tom is tired after working long hours. On these days, he is sometimes aloof or short with her. In response, she gets angry and tells him to stop taking his job stress out on her. This creates a fight that often repeats itself in their relationship.

If you were teaching this skill to Jenny, first you would ask her to examine the thoughts she has when she notices Tom in a bad mood. She might say, "I worry that he doesn't love me or that he doesn't care." She might also say, "I wonder what I did wrong." You will notice that these thoughts are negative and keep her from making choices confidently. After identifying these thoughts, you would encourage her to develop some neutral or positive replacement thoughts such as, "Maybe Tom is having a bad day," or "his stress may have nothing to do with me." Another example could include, "Even if he is stressed by something I am doing, he will need to let me know when he is ready. He's clearly not ready right now."

After using cognitive restructuring, you can encourage Jenny to either do some self-care or to ask for her needs in an appropriate way. For example, if Tom really just needs some alone time, Jenny could do some self-care such as engage in a hobby or even take a long, relaxing bath. Her night does not have to be a bad one just because Tom is stressed. Oppositely, if Tom snapped at her, she may wait a moment until the night is calmer, then state a boundary such as, "Hey Tom, I get that you were in a bad mood tonight. I just ask that next time you give me a heads up so I can give you some space. I would rather you ask me for space then snap at me." Whether Jenny takes care of her own needs or asks for help from her partner, the key aspect of this skill is to guide Jenny in being more proactive and less reactive. Targeting her thoughts can be a helpful tool to encourage her assertiveness.

Effective versus Ineffective Ways to ask for Needs and Wants

Most couples could benefit from learning how to ask for their needs and wants in an effective way. There are clearly approaches that work well and approaches that do not work very well. Couples often use approaches that make it difficult to get their needs and wants met. For example, Angie may yell, "put the trash out when you are done!" to her partner, Jeffrey. While he may still take out the trash, over time this approach can get tiring and produce the opposite effect. Later in the relationship, Jeffrey might retort, "Do it yourself," because he gets tired of being ordered around. Whereas, if she asked, "Hey babe, can you please take out the trash?" over time he may be more willing to follow through with her requests because he feels respected.

In a pre-marital session, I teach this skill by drawing a line down the middle of my white board. At the top of each section I write, "Effective" and "Ineffective." Then, I ask clients to identify specific approaches they know to be ineffective for them personally and to identify specific approaches that work best for them personally. I write my client's examples under each list. This is helpful because individuals differ in terms of what approaches work best for them. Ideally, it is important to encourage each person to use the approach their partner prefers. For more information, I also encourage couples to read *Why Marriages Succeed or Fail* (Gottmann, 1995) to learn about how they can soften their approaches to each other.

Rookie Mistakes

One common mistake couples make is to put all responsibility for needs and wants on their partner or blame their partner when things are not going as planned. The truth is, in most situations, each partner has choices they can make to improve the situation or to make the situation worse. For example, Sam and Dana often fought about unmet needs in the relationship. When things weren't going well, Sam often blamed Dana for not being available or spending quality time with him. However, upon further assessment, I recognized that Sam would never tell Dana he wanted more time with her until after he was extremely angry about the situation. By the time Dana got the message, it was a big fight.

In every session, I try to help clients take more responsibility for their personal actions and inactions. While Sam may be right about Dana putting their relationship last at times, it could be helpful to encourage Sam to ask for time together more often and at a time when the relationship is *not* in crisis. When you have a client who tends to put the blame on others, you could potentially say, "I noticed many of your answers are pointing to your partner's choices. While it is important for you to be honest about your concerns, it is equally important for you two to look at the role you personally play. You can't control your partner's actions, but you can control your own. How can you do things differently?" By encouraging individuals to take personal responsibility, you can help them to take more control in their relationships.

Another common mistake you may find with your couples includes one or both partners being very defensive when it comes to bringing up needs and wants. For example, Terry and Jim discussed the best approaches to use to ask for things. I noticed Jim struggled with approaches that most people would consider respectful. When I suggested they try using the phrase, "Would you mind doing _____ for me," Jim replied that request seemed very critical. Terry added that she struggled to find good ways to ask him for things. Even when she tried to ask nicely, he still struggled to take the feedback. In this example, Jim may have a high level of defensiveness. In a situation like this, a clinician should point this out and work with Jim on how he can be more accepting of feedback, especially when it is given respectfully.

One final pitfall you may encounter includes clients who are largely unaware of what they may need or want in any given situation. One way to guide clients to learn more about their needs is to encourage them to recognize and attend to their own emotions. Emotions exist to help us make decisions about different situations. "From an evolutionary perspective, emotions are adaptations that track important costs and benefits in the environment and adjust behavior in ways that increase the individual's capacity and tendency to respond adaptively" (Ellis and Malamuth, 2000, p. 527). For example, fear helps us to spring into action. A person may feel afraid and need to get out of a dangerous situation. To teach clients to better identify their needs, first you can help them identify a specific feeling they are experiencing. Second, you can help them identify what unmet need may be associated with that feeling.

For example, Madge commonly ignored her emotions. She was taught to move on and get over things quickly. However, lately she had felt very uneasy with her life. I explained to her the importance of recognizing emotions and asked her to identify what emotion she was experiencing: anxious/worried, frustrated, angry, sad, disgusted, happy, etc. Madge stated it might be worry. Once we identified the emotion, I asked her to consider what unmet need may be associated with her anxiety. She stated that it felt like too many things in her life needed attention. She was overwhelmed with all her responsibilities. I then encouraged her to look at the people in her life to see whether she could get some outside help to manage all the tasks at hand.

For each couple that comes into pre-marital counseling, it is important for clinicians to guide individuals in how to identify their personal needs and effectively communicate this information with their partners. If both partners are working to meet each other's needs, they can be happier in their lives as a married couple.

Practice Ideas

1. Do some research on different therapeutic models such as "emotion-focused couples therapy" that discuss meeting needs in

relationships. Find a few interventions that more specifically teach clients how to effectively identify and meet their own needs.

2. Practice identifying what deeper need or want a client is asking for in sessions. Many times, people are discussing topics at a surface level. Try to identify and state out loud the needs each person is trying to convey.

3. When you personally are experiencing an emotion, try to identify what need is not being met in yourself. Do something to actively meet this need.

Bibliography

American Psychiatric Association (2013). *Diagnostic and Statistical Manual of Mental Disorders*, 5th Ed. Arlington, VA: American Psychiatric Association.

Covey, S.R. (2004). *The 7 Habits of Highly Effective People*. New York: Simon & Schuster.

Crystal, B. (1995). *Forget Paris*. Castle Rock Entertainment.

Ellis, B.J. and Malamuth, N.M. (2000). Love and Anger in Romantic Relationships: A Discrete Systems Model. *Journal of Personality*, *68*(3), 525–556.

Evans, M. (2004). Cognitive restructuring: CBT vs ISD. *Telesur*, October 23, www.telesurtv.net/english/opinion/Cognitive-Restructuring-CBT-vs-ISD--20141023-0081.html.

Ghose, T. (2013). History of Marriage: 13 Surprising Facts. *Live Science, Fox News:* Tech Media Network Company, June 27, www.foxnews.com/health/2013/06/27/history-marriage-13-surprising-facts.

Gottman, J. (1995). *Why Marriages Succeed or Fail*. New York: Simon & Schuster.

Gurman, A.S. (2008). *Clinical Handbook of Couple Therapy*, 4th ed. New York: The Guilford Press.

Johnson, S.J. (2004). *Emotionally Focused Couple Therapy with Trauma Survivors: Strengthening Attachment Bonds*. New York: The Guilford Press.

Markel, P. (2014). Maslow knew prepping: Understanding the Hierarchy of Needs in the 21st Century. *The Blaze*, April 14, www.theblaze.com/contributions/maslow-knew-prepping-understanding-the-hierarchy-of-needs-in-the-21st-century-4.

Session Six

KEEPING THE
SPARK ALIVE

Ten years from now you're gonna be having sex with your wife. And it's gonna be in the missionary position. And one of you is going to be asleep.

Jake Johnson, *No Strings Attached*

In the 2014 pilot episode of *Married*, the main couple sits in bed. The husband is exploring himself while she is busy reading a book. He states there is something weird happening with his penis. He invites his wife to touch it. She ignores him. He goes on to state that his penis may even taste interesting and she should try it. At this, he hears a resounding "No" from his partner. This example is a common view of American married sex. Our culture views married sex as bland, boring, and in many cases non-existent (especially after having kids). Even though most married couples do not want this to be their fate.

Keeping the spark alive is the fifth habit for successful marriages. Many couples will report a brief honeymoon period that lasts anywhere from 6 months to 2 years within the beginning of the relationship. After that period, it can be a downhill slope leading to less and less sex if couples don't keep working at it. In 15–20 percent of marriages, couples are having sex as little as 10 times a year or less (*Newsweek*, 2014). In her 2012 recap of the book, *The Secret Lives of Wives: Women share what it really takes to stay married*, Iris Krasnow reported that most of the women she interviewed reported that keeping a dynamic sex life was a key component to keeping their marital lives strong over time. Contrarily, many relationships that did not maintain their intimacy ended in divorce.

In order to keep the spark alive, an individual needs to know what sparks desire for himself or herself, to communicate this information clearly to their partner, and to take action by engaging in erotic activities that increase desire for their partner. Second, an individual needs to be in a relationship in which their partner is open to exploring these various sexual interests as a consensual team. Finally, both partners must commit to working at this part of the relationship consistently over time. Without consistent work in this area, many couples will experience sexless marriages as a natural result of being in a relationship long term.

Myths about Sex

The way our culture understands sex has changed. Thanks to revolutionary researchers such as William Masters, Virginia Johnson, and Alfred Kinsey, to name a few, what we know about sex has come a long way. Stereotypes have been debunked, newer understandings about sexual function and dysfunction have been researched, and the general population is becoming more aware of how to handle and treat sexual issues.

Even with this new information, there are still misunderstandings about some of these sexual issues and a lack of knowledge for where clients should turn to seek help. There are also misunderstandings still about what is considered to be sexually normal and even healthy in a relationship. In this section, I will go over some common myths that are contributing to sexual problems for couples.

Myth #1: Once I am in a committed relationship, I should not have to masturbate. My sexual relationship should be enough to fulfill me.

Reality: In many relationships, sex can be very fulfilling and require less masturbation. However, if an individual expects their partner to meet all of their sexual needs, they will likely be let down. Commonly, two partners will not have the same sexual desire levels—one person may desire sex once daily while the other desires sex once weekly. Masturbation can sometimes be used in these situations to fulfill sexual needs when couples aren't similar in their desire levels. In a British National Survey of Sexual Attitudes and Lifestyles (NATSAL), the study found that commonly men used masturbation as a way to compensate for not getting as much vaginal sex as they would prefer (Gerressu et al., 2008). As long as a couple reports fulfillment with their mutual sex life, it is perfectly reasonable for one or both partners to use masturbation in addition to sex as a means to fulfill sexual desires when the other party is not in the mood for sex.

In addition, masturbation is a great way to figure out what techniques help an individual get an orgasm. Self-exploration allows women and men to learn about their personal desires and interests. From this information, they can communicate their desires to their partner. Then the couple can use this information to enhance their sexual relationship.

Myth #2: Women and men should orgasm in every sexual experience. Sex is not worth it if you don't orgasm.

Reality: While it is enjoyable to reach orgasm, it does not have to be a requirement for good sex. Sex is about having a fun and pleasurable experience with a partner. Orgasm is the by-product of having fun, using a few useful techniques, and being in the moment sexually with your partner. Couples who put too much pressure on reaching orgasm can struggle to reach orgasms over time. It is common for Sex Therapists to teach couples to shift the focus of sex to pleasure, playfulness, and mutual relaxation as a means to reduce the symptoms of sexual dysfunction.

Another reason to shift the focus of sex to pleasure is that some women struggle to reach orgasm during penetrative sex. Many women are not "anatomically constructed to receive clitoral stimulation during vaginal intercourse" (Bancroft and Graham, 2011, p. 721). Most women need clitoral stimulation to achieve orgasm. Couples can engage in this type of stimulation using other methods, such as oral sex or digital stimulation.

The couple that puts more focus on sex for pleasure is likely to be more flexible in their approach to love making. This means they will be able to make out, pleasure their partner solely, or even focus on sensual massage and just enjoy that experience, regardless of whether they get to orgasm. Sometimes, these actions will lead to orgasms. However, a willingness to just focus on enjoying the moment will allow these couples to enjoy whatever sexual experience they engage in regardless of the outcome.

Myth #3: My partner should know what will please me sexually. If they don't know, it is their job to figure it out.

Reality: It is both partners' responsibility to figure out what will please themselves and their partner. Individuals who have this expectation going into their sexual relationship are often unhappy with the outcome. It is first the job of the individual to learn what they personally enjoy. From this information, they can guide their partner to please them sexually. For women who have never experienced orgasm, it is common for a sex therapist to suggest that a woman first learn to self-pleasure to reach orgasm. From this self-exploration, she can learn what types of fantasies, touch, pacing, and techniques work best for her. Then, she can guide her partner to try the techniques she has learned.

If there is no sexual exploration individually, it can be very hard for a partner to try and figure out what makes that individual feel good. I have often seen couples in which the wife will tell her husband everything he is doing wrong, but never guides him in what feels good. When he asks about what she likes, she will say she doesn't know. This tends to leave her husband feeling frustrated and defeated. In essence, it is the individual's responsibility to learn what they like and communicate these likes to their partner. Over time, their partner will learn what pleases them sexually and engage in these actions intentionally without having to be asked.

Myth #4: It is the man's job to initiate sex. Men typically have a higher libido and should therefore initiate more.

Reality: Libido and desire are very unique qualities to each individual. Sometimes, the man is the person with the higher libido and tends to initiate more. Sometimes, the woman is the person with the higher libido. Rather than putting all the pressure on one person to initiate, both partners should ensure a regular frequency of sex (Metz and McCarthy, 2012). Couples can discuss what their ideal sex life should look like and each make efforts to initiate at a frequency that both parties agree to.

It is also important to remember that desire can change over time. Each person is responsible for maintaining their personal desire levels. Throughout a person's lifespan, there are common times when desire is lower and higher. For example, most people have higher desire levels in their teens and twenties. However, right after having a baby, it is common for a new mom to have a reduced desire for sex due to changes in her hormones and exhaustion from the new baby. In another example, many women have very high desire in their late 30s and 40s. At the same time, men's desire begins to slow down toward their 40s and 50s. Regardless of who has the higher desire level, both parties need to make a conscious effort to maintain their personal desire level or at least achieve a level of sexual satisfaction both parties agree to.

Myth #5: If one partner has a sexual dysfunction, this means sex will need to stop for a time.

Reality: There will be many times in a couples' life where different things can get in the way of sex. Common sexual dysfunctions include erectile dysfunction, premature ejaculation, low desire or desire disorder, orgasmic dysfunction, and female pelvic pain during sex. When one individual suffers from a sexual dysfunction, it is very important for the couple to find alternative ways to be intimate while they receive treatment for their conditions.

Couples can use sexual massage, oral sex, digital stimulation, cuddling, kissing/making out, role playing, sex toys, and various other possible techniques to enjoy an intimate life together. The key is for the couple to make a commitment to meeting each other's sexual needs despite obstacles and to seek treatment when needed. Instead of stopping sex, couples can shift sex to accommodate the new situation.

Teaching Couples to Create a Dynamite Sex Life

There are a few important tools couples need to create a healthy sex life: 1) communication that is relaxed and positive; 2) an ability to take personal responsibility for one's needs and desires; 3) a relationship in which both partners value each other and try to incorporate their partners' sexual needs and desires.

In her video, Esther Perrel discussed how couples need to find a balance between the selfish and the selfless (Perrel, 2006). In order to be sexually satisfied, an individual must pursue their own sexual interests while also pursuing their partner's sexual interests. Sex is selfish in that an individual needs to know what they want and desire. They need to learn what types of things turn them on sexually and feel confident in seeking these things from their partner. Sex is selfless in how partners respond to one another. In a selfless relationship, an individual learns about their partner's needs and actively tries to incorporate these desires into their sex life. They develop an attitude of willingness which helps their partner to keep sharing their desires. This combination creates a space for a dynamic sex life.

In the following interventions, clinicians can find a few ideas for how to teach healthy sexual concepts to their clients. Sexual health is vital to a couple's marriage health, and clinicians are in a great position to educate pre-marital clients so couples can start things out on the right foot. I encourage clinicians to develop their own personal courage in this area by seeking additional training in sex therapy if needed.

Responsible Desire

There are different types of desire that are commonly discussed in the literature—spontaneous desire and responsive desire. Spontaneous desire refers to a general feeling of arousal that seemingly comes out of nowhere. For example, a young adolescent boy sitting in the classroom may randomly get an erection without warning. In another example, a woman may be in the shower and suddenly begin feeling aroused. This type of desire refers to a person's base level of desire or arousal—meaning how often they typically begin to feel sexual. Each person experiences spontaneous desire at different rates. For example, some people have this type of desire daily, while others experience it once a month or even less.

Contrarily, responsive desire is defined as a subjective arousal to a sexual stimulus that then triggers a person's desire or arousal (Basson,

2007). For example, John may not have been thinking about sex. When his partner Susan starts rubbing his lower back, he quickly becomes aroused by her interest in sex with him. In another example, a woman may be reading a book and read a sexy scene. In response to the scene, she gets aroused. Many women report they do not experience spontaneous desire as much as they experience responsive desire. These women may not initiate sex as frequently as their male counterparts, because they tend to experience desire in response to their partner's interest in sex.

This difference in desire can cause problems for couples for various reasons. For example, Jane tends to only experience responsive desire. John, her husband, complains that she never wants to have sex because she never initiates. This has led him to avoid initiating sex altogether at times to wait and see how long it would take before she would try to have sex with him. However, this strategy has left him very unhappy. Many times she could wait from weeks to months before initiating sex. Jane states that she has no problem getting into sex once he tries, but he never tries anymore. In this example, this couple could likely benefit from understanding the difference between the types of desire and learning to work with each other's desire as a team.

As a sex therapist, I often advocate for women and men to engage in something called "responsible desire," in which they each learn what turns them on personally and actively engage in thoughts or actions that can turn themselves on. This can be a helpful skill because there are times in married life when desire can be low for one or both partners. If both partners are experiencing low desire, then sex can stop for long periods of time and create distance between the partners. As in the example with Jane and John, John waited for Jane to experience desire spontaneously instead of doing things to spark her responsive desire. While Jane was unaware that John would do this, she also could have benefitted from intentionally putting herself in the mood and then initiating sex with her partner on a more regular basis.

In pre-marital counseling, I encourage counselors to teach partners how to take responsibility for their own desire. Clinicians can guide clients in discussing what specific things arouse each partner openly. After they each have learned some of the things that tend to work, clinicians can encourage clients to actively create personal desire and initiate sex with their partner. Examples of things that couples may enjoy include romantic dates, sexy lingerie, sex toys, role playing, certain books and movies, staying in hotel rooms, wine, flirting, etc. After identifying examples, clinicians would have the couple practice intentionally doing some of the activities to practice creating desire at least once a week or even more. If ever the couple experienced a low desire period later in their relationship, they could practice using this tool again intentionally to improve desire.

Good Enough Sex Model

In the American culture, there are many depictions of sex that are negative or problematic. Television shows exist about sex addicts, sexual problems, and various fetishes that people would deem strange. However, what our culture commonly lacks is a model for what healthy sex should look like in a relationship. The Good Enough Sex Model (Metz and McCarthy, 2012) is one model couples can use to learn about healthy sexuality.

Couples need a healthy sex model so they can feel normal. In my Sex, Wine and Chocolate seminars, I offer a question-and-answer section in which individuals can give me anonymous questions about sex that I will answer candidly. I often find that most questions have a very similar theme: Am I normal? Giving couples a sexual health model can help them to feel normal and comfortable talking about their sexual needs and desires with their partners.

Clinicians can use this model as the main teaching tool in the session by going over each of the 12 principles listed in the Good Enough Sex Model and having a discussion with the couple about how the principles relate to their own sex lives. The 12 principles can be found in the book *New Directions in Sex Therapy* (Metz and McCarthy, 2012). The principles are as follows:

1. Sex is a good element in life, an invaluable part of an individual's and a couple's long-term comfort, intimacy, pleasure, and confidence. Eroticism is an intentional feature and the responsibility of each partner.

2. Relationship and sexual satisfaction are the ultimate developmental focus and are essentially intertwined. "The couple is an intimate team" and together promote a vibrant balance of emotional intimacy and eroticism.

3. Accurate, realistic, and age-appropriate physiological, psychological relationships and sexual expectations are essential for sexual satisfaction.

4. Good physical health and healthy behavioral habits are vital for sexual health. Each individual values, respects, and affirms his/her partner's sexual body.

5. Relaxation is the foundation for pleasure and function.

6. Pleasure is as important as function.

7. Valuing variable, flexible sexual experiences and abandoning the "need" for perfect performance inoculates the couple against sexual dysfunction by reducing performance pressure, fears of failure, and rejection.

8. Five basic purposes for sex (pleasure, intimacy, stress reduction, self-esteem, and reproduction) are integrated into the couple's sexual relationship. Sex for only one purpose for extended periods of time (i.e. fertility) undermines flexibility and creates the risk of sexual dysfunction and distress.

9. Integrate and flexibly use the three basic sexual arousal styles (sensual self-entrancement, partner interaction, and role enactment).

10. Partner gender differences and preferences are respectfully valued and similarities mutually accepted. Partners cooperate as an intimate team for relationship and sexual pleasure and satisfaction.

11. Sex is integrated into real life and real life is integrated into sex. Partners ensure a regular frequency of sex. Sexuality is developing, growing, and evolving throughout one's life to create a unique sexual style. Regularity ensures an emotional "intimacy blender".

12. Sexuality is personalized: sex can be playful, spiritual, "special."

I will have clients read the principles one by one in session and discuss each in detail. I ask questions such as, "Do you agree or disagree with this principle and why?" or "What does this principle mean for you?" or "What examples in your life connect with this principle?"

The session typically focuses on helping the couple develop a mutually agreeable definition of what healthy sexuality looks like in their relationship. I like using the model because it is an easy way to start a conversation about sex and what it means to each partner. The key to a good conversation is to be non-judgmental and encourage clients to do the same when listening to their partner's opinions.

Sexual Dysfunctions Overview

Mike and Charla came into therapy after several years of coping with a sexless marriage. I had asked them where the problem started. Charla replied that sex started to hurt after they had their baby. When the pain didn't go away, she began avoiding sex. She talked about it with her doctor and he stated she should use Crisco. When the Crisco didn't work, she started avoiding sex.

It is very common in my practice to work with clients who are experiencing very real sexual dysfunctions such as painful sex or female pain/penetration disorder. Due to lack of knowledge about potential treatments, they learn to just live with the problem rather than improving it. Often, the way an individual copes with a sexual dysfunction is to avoid sex. This action does not lead to a satisfying marital life.

One very helpful thing a pre-marital counselor can do is give information about the common sexual dysfunctions: erectile dysfunction, premature ejaculation, low desire, painful sexual intercourse, and orgasmic disorder. Clinicians can offer some basic information about the disorders and suggest books that give helpful information. One key feature is to encourage the couple to talk openly about any disorders if and when they happen and to be committed to seeking treatment. Another helpful guideline is to let them know there are many treatment options available including medical therapies, physical therapies, and sex therapies. Finally, clinicians can encourage couples to develop their own plan of action should sexual problems occur.

If you are not familiar with the sexual dysfunctions, I will briefly address three of the most common I see in my own practice. For further information beyond my discussion in this chapter, helpful books to read include the DSM-5 section on sexual dysfunctions, *Principles and Practice of Sex Therapy* by Sandra Leiblum, and *New Directions in Sex Therapy* by Peggy Kleinplatz.

Painful Sexual Intercourse

A very common sexual problem couples will address is Genito-Pelvic Pain/Penetration Disorder. In the DSM-5, this disorder has the following symptoms (American Psychiatric Association, 2013, p. 437).

> *Persistent or recurrent difficulties with one or more of the following:*
> 1. *Vaginal penetration during intercourse.*
> 2. *Marked . . . pelvic pain during vaginal intercourse or penetration attempts.*
> 3. *Marked fear or anxiety about . . . pelvic pain in anticipation of, during or as a result of vaginal penetration.*
> 4. *Marked tensing or tightening of the pelvic floor muscles during attempted vaginal penetration.*

For more information, please see the DSM-5 directly for a more complete listing of additional criteria and diagnostic features.

According to a recent study by the Center for Sexual Health Promotion by Indiana University, around 30 percent of all women between the ages of 18 and 59 have experienced painful sex at some point in their lives (Firger, 2014). This means that at some point in your career working with couples, you will likely encounter women who are suffering from painful sexual intercourse that is affecting their current sex life.

The challenge for our clients is to educate them on the reality of this problem and to encourage them to seek effective, helpful treatment. Since it is such a common disorder, clinicians can start by normalizing this problem during pre-marital counseling. I usually start the conversation by saying, "Painful sex is a common sexual problem women experience. Some of the key times it may occur during your sex life include after a pregnancy, during or after menopause, or during periods of sickness/illness. The most important thing about any sexual problem is to remember to be honest with each other and to seek treatment."

Starting this conversation can also open the door for the couple if the partner is currently experiencing painful sex. Some women will experience it as early as their first sexual experiences. If your client is currently experiencing painful sex, remind them that they are not "broken." People have all kinds of problems throughout their lives—sexual, medical, and mental. The key to getting past these problems is open communication and mutual support.

Next, discuss the most effective treatment options for this kind of problem. Since painful sex is considered both a physical and mental disorder, the best course of treatment is a collaborative approach that includes a few resources. First, a medical doctor who specializes in this type of treatment can be helpful, such as an obstetrics and gynecologist (OBGYN) or urologist. Medical professionals can offer medications, topical creams, and referrals to physical therapy. If a woman has discussed this issue with her OBGYN, and they haven't offered referrals or resources, then encourage your client to seek a new OBGYN. Not all doctors are trained to help with sexual dysfunctions, even if they specialize in gynecology.

Second, a female pelvic floor physical therapist is specially trained to work through the pain expressed through the muscle tissue in the vagina. Pelvic floor physical therapists will offer specific exercises to strengthen the area, stretching exercises, and various other techniques that help a woman relax these muscles.

Finally, a sex therapist can help couples keep their sex life going well while working through the medical and physical therapy treatments. Often, the treatment for painful sex can take some time. The average treatment length can last from 12 to 20 weeks, depending on various factors involved in the woman's assessment. During this time, some couples struggle to be intimate at all. A helpful sex therapist will work with the other professionals to find ways to incorporate the treatment into a couple's sex life. They may also encourage the couple to use alternative means to be intimate such as foreplay, cuddling, oral sex, toys, or any other means the couple is willing to use.

Erectile Dysfunction

Another sexual problem couples face is erectile dysfunction. Some of the common symptoms listed in the DSM-5 for this problem include (American Psychiatric Association, 2013, p. 426):

> *At least one of the three following symptoms must be experienced on almost all or all (approximately 75–100 percent) occasions of sexual activity. . . :*
>
> 1. *Marked difficulty in obtaining an erection during sexual activity.*
> 2. *Marked difficulty in maintaining an erection until the completion of sexual activity.*
> 3. *Marked decrease in erectile rigidity.*

For more information, please see the DSM-5 directly for a more complete listing of additional criteria and diagnostic features.

It is quite common for men to experience some level of erection problems at different stages of their lives. While not all men will actually get a diagnosis of erectile dysfunction, every now and then an erection is not going to be perfect, and it is important not to view these occasional mishaps as total failures. Metz and McCarthy (2004) reported that 15 percent of the time, sex can be downright dysfunctional for either party involved. Since sex will not always be perfect, it is normal for there to be some sexual experiences in which a male loses his erection. The key is for couples to find effective ways to address these inconvenient sexual interchanges in a positive, productive way.

Some factors that contribute to erection problems include excessive drinking, obesity, medical illnesses, disability, certain medications, sexually transmitted infections, and high levels of stress (Metz and McCarthy, 2004). Medications to look out for include psychotropic medicines, muscle relaxers, and pain medications. Clients can check the side effects for specific medications they are currently taking to see if there may be sexual side effects. Please note that it is important that clients work with their medical professionals to find a medication that best supports their medical needs and sexual needs. It is not advised for clients to abruptly end use of a medication without consulting their physician.

In addition, there are some valuable life choices men can make to improve erectile function. For example, living a healthy life style can promote healthy erections. A healthy life style includes regular exercise, no smoking, limited drinking, and a healthy diet that includes fruits, vegetables, and proteins.

One helpful method for discussing this problem with pre-marital clients is to discuss when it commonly takes place and what types of treatment are available. It is common for men after 50 to begin having erection problems that need more medical help. There are several treatments available that include medications such as Viagra and Cialis. In addition to medical treatment, sex therapy can be a helpful treatment. Couples will learn valuable skills for how to work better as a team to reduce anxiety around erection problems and to keep sex fun and enjoyable.

It is common for people to use medications such as Viagra or Cialis and still have some erection difficulty for various reasons. One reason the medication may not work involves a couple's interaction patterns around the erectile dysfunction. For example, Tom and Susan had grown very angry with each other about sex. Tom knew he had erection problems and initially avoided initiating sex with Susan. This left Susan worrying that he was cheating on her with another woman. After some time, Tom secretly went to a doctor to get Viagra. When he tried to initiate, his wife was not interested because she didn't trust him.

One of the best skills a pre-marital counselor can give to their clients is a method for directly addressing sexual problems with each other. This method includes first normalizing sexual problems: "At some point in your lives, one of you is likely to experience a sexual issue. How do you want to bring these issues up with each other?" From this question, guide your couples in creating an action plan for how they bring up their sexual problems, how they can best respond, and what they will do to seek help.

Low Desire

Another common problem clients face is low desire. This is called Female Sexual Interest/Arousal Disorder in women and Male Hypoactive

Sexual Desire Disorder in men. Research on desire is still relatively new. Sexual interest and desire can be very different depending on gender, biological predisposition, socio-cultural factors, and relational interaction patterns. In this section, we will focus mainly on female sexual desire problems. However, I encourage all clinicians to familiarize themselves with the symptoms for both disorders.

The symptoms from the DSM-5 for Female Sexual Interest/Arousal Disorder include (American Psychiatric Association, 2013, p. 433):

Lack of, or significantly reduced, sexual interest/arousal, as manifested by at least three of the following:

1. *Absent/reduced interest in sexual activity.*
2. *Absent/reduced sexual/erotic thoughts or fantasies.*
3. *No/reduced initiation of sexual activity, and typically unreceptive to a partner's attempts to initiate.*
4. *Absent/reduced sexual excitement/pleasure during sexual activity . . .*
5. *Absent/reduced sexual interest/arousal in response to . . . erotic cues.*
6. *Absent/reduced genital or non-genital sensations during sexual activities . . .*

For more information, please see the DSM-5 directly for a more complete listing of additional criteria and diagnostic features.

While low desire in the female is a common diagnosis that couples come into therapy for, there are often unrealistic expectations couples present with regarding what sexual desire should look like in the married relationship. In pre-marital counseling, we are in a key position to help couples set realistic expectations with each other.

For starters, it is commonly the woman in the relationship who has lower desire (Laumann et al., 1999; Carvalho and Nobre, 2011). However, in every sexual relationship, there are discrepancies between parties about when desire is present. In his book *Passionate Marriage*, David Schnarch (2009) proposes that in every marriage there is a high-desire partner and a low-desire partner. While it typically tends to be the woman, I have seen a variety of couples where the man is the low-desire partner. In cases of same-sex marriage, there is still one person who is the lower-desire partner.

As clinicians, try to normalize sexual desire differences whether they come from the male or the female in the relationship. We can teach our clients the difference between an actual desire disorder and the natural variations that occur between individuals in a couple.

Second, clinicians can guide couples to come up with compromises for how to address these differences. In the previous section about responsible desire, I offered some specific options for how couples can intentionally put themselves in the mood and ensure regular sex by taking turns initiating. In addition, couples can also read some helpful books that are meant to guide couples in creating an open dialogue about sex. These books include David Schnarch's *Passionate Marriage*, Esther Perrel's *Mating in Captivity*, Paul Joannides' *The Guide to Getting it On*, and Dr. Kevin Leman's *Sex Begins in the Kitchen*. The books offer examples of different ways that couples can increase their personal and relational desire. They are helpful guides for how couples can begin to address desire differences as a team.

Rookie Mistakes

Most clients want to discuss their sex life with clinicians but can be too afraid to bring it up on their own. Often clients will take their cues from the therapist as to what issues can and cannot be discussed. If the clinician never brings up sex, the clients will stay and work for a while on couple issues, but then eventually move on to a different therapist to discuss their sexual issues. For this reason, it can be helpful to bring up sex relatively early in pre-marital counseling so couples know it is an acceptable topic to discuss.

Another common mistake couples make is thinking that working on the relationship solely will help them improve their sex life. In her book, *Mating in Captivity*, Esther Perrel (2006) discusses a group of couples in therapy that report being very close friends and very connected emotionally. Despite feeling very close as friends, they do not have a great sex life. Perrell suggests that there are in fact two separate treatment tracks, the sexual relationship and the friendship, that do not necessarily interrelate. Having a good friendship does not mean a couple will have a good sex life.

For example, Tina and John were the nicest, most considerate people I had ever met. They were great friends and great at listening to each other. This kindness made it difficult for them to be assertive about their desires. Tina would be interested in sex, but notice John was busy working on his computer. Since she did not want to interrupt him, she would busy herself with some other task. Similarly, John might be interested in sex. When Tina stated she was tired, he assumed she wanted to go to bed when in reality, a couple of times, she had been insinuating they could go to bed early to be intimate. He did not pick up on her cues because they weren't direct. Over time, their consideration for each other had led to less sex between them than they both preferred.

In order to avoid this mistake, clinicians should treat the emotional relationship and the sexual relationship as two separate tracts. In my own treatment plans, I create separate sections for sexual interventions and intimacy building interventions. The sexual interventions focus on ways to increase excitement/desire, ways to help the couple take risks, and ways for clients to build a sexual language. I normalize sexual differences and try to help couples find compromises that meet both partners' sexual needs and desires. Most of all, I normalize sexual fantasies so clients will feel confident in sharing.

Another mistake clients make is discussing sex angrily or using very negative language. Some pre-marital couples come into therapy very frustrated about the state of their sex life. While it is good for them to explain their frustrations to you, keeping a negative dialogue around sex long term will decrease desire for sex. Clinicians must change the style of dialogue early in therapy to a more accepting and respectful tone. Clinicians can do this by explaining how delicate the topic of sex can be for any individual. Such a delicate topic requires respect in and out of sessions to really make an impact. From there, clinicians can guide couples in creating rules around how to talk about sex both inside and outside of sessions. These rules can be created by the clients and include options such as, "Be willing to listen to your partner, even if you disagree," or "Don't argue after a session. Take time to think and discuss it when you are both calm." Clinicians can even ask clients how they prefer to enforce the rules they create to establish further accountability.

Keeping the spark alive is a habit that needs to be consistently worked on. As a pre-marital clinician, a big part of our job is to establish healthy sexual habits in the beginning of the relationship. At the end of this session, be sure to remind your clients that this is meant to be a lifelong journey. A couples' sex life ebbs and flows across time, getting more intense and less intense at different times. The key is to keep improving upon it and to help couples develop a way to address their sex life productively when they do crave more.

Practice Ideas

1. Read any of the following books to familiarize yourself with some helpful sex therapy tools: *Sex Begins in the Kitchen*, by Dr. Kevin Leman; *The Guide to Getting it On*, by Paul Joannides; *Mating in Captivity*, by Esther Perrel; *Becoming Orgasmic*, by J.R. Heiman and J. LoPiccolo; *New Directions in Sex Therapy*, by Peggy Kleinplatz. Encourage your couples to read chapters in these books together weekly and practice the activities in each section.

2. Practice using the Sexual History Questionnaire with your clients. This assessment is a great tool to learn more about clients' sex lives.

3. Take some continuing education courses in sex therapy. Any clinician who works with couples will have to address sex at some point. It is best to be educated in this area so you can offer help. If you want to get certified, the American Association for Sex Educators, Counselors, and Therapists (AASECT) offers a national certification in Sex Therapy.

Bibliography

American Psychiatric Association (Ed.) (2013). Sexual Dysfunctions. In *Diagnostic and Statistical Manual of Mental Disorders (DSM-5)*, 5th ed. Washington, DC: American Psychiatric Publishing, pp. 423–450.

Ashford, M. (2013 to Present). *Masters of Sex*. Showtime.

Bancroft, J. and Graham, C.A. 2011. The varied nature of women's sexuality: Unresolved issues and a theoretical approach. *Hormones and Behavior, 59*, 717–729.

Basson, R. (2007). Sexual Desire/Arousal Disorders in Women. In S.R. Leiblum (Ed.), *Principles and Practice of Sex Therapy*, 4th ed. New York: The Guilford Press, pp. 25–53.

Carvalho, J. and Nobre, P. (2011). Gender differences in sexual desire: How do emotional and relationship factors determine sexual desire according to gender? *Sexologies, 20,* 207–211.

Firger, J. (July, 2014). Pain during Sex: What Women need to Know. CBS News. CBS Interactive, www.cbsnews.com/news/pain-during-sex-what-women-need-to-know.

Gerressu, M., Mercer, C.H., Graham, C.A., Wellings, K., and Johnson, A.M. (2008). Prevalence of Masturbation and Associated Factors from a British National probability survey. *Archives of Sexual Behavior, 37,* 266–278.

Gurland, A. (2014 to Present). *Married.* FX.

Heiman, J. and LoPiccolo, J. (1987). *Becoming Orgasmic.* Jouve, France: Prentice Hall.

Joannides, P. and Gross, D. (2013). *The Guide to Getting it On.* Saline, MI: Goofy Foot.

Kleinplatz, P.J. (2012). *New Directions in Sex Therapy: Innovations and Alternatives.* New York: Routledge.

Krasnow, I. (2011). *The Secret Lives of Wives: Women share what it really takes to stay married.* New York: Penguin Group.

Krasnow, I. (2012). Good Sex Makes for a Lasting Marriage. *Huffington Post,* December 8, www.huffingtonpost.com/iris-krasnow/good-sex-makes-for-a-lasting_b_1949760.html.

Laumann, E.O., Paik, A., and Rosen, R.C. (1999). Sexual dysfunction in the United States: Prevalence and predictors, *Journal of the American Medical Association, 281,* 537–544.

Leiblum, S.R. (2007). *Principles and Practice of Sex Therapy,* 4th ed. New York: The Guilford Press.

Leman, K. (2006). *Sex Begins in the Kitchen.* Grand Rapids, MI: Revell.

Metz, M.E. and McCarthy, B.W. (2004). *Coping with Erectile Dysfunction: How to Regain Confidence and Enjoy Great Sex.* Oakland, CA: New Harbinger.

Metz, M.E. and McCarthy, B.W. (2012). The Good Enough Sex (GES) model: Perspective and clinical applications. In P.J. Kleinplatz (Ed.), *New directions in sex therapy: Innovations and alternatives* (2nd ed.), 213–230. New York: Routledge.

Newsweek (2014). No sex, please we're married. *PRNewswire,* June, www.prnewswire.com/news-releases/newsweek-cover-no-sex-please-were-married-71373437.html.

Perrel, E. (2006). *Mating in Captivity: Unlocking Erotic Intelligence.* New York: HarperCollins.

Perrel, E. (2013). *The Secret to Desire in a Long Term Relationship.* TED talks, YouTube, February.

Reitman, I. (2011). *No Strings Attached.* Paramount Pictures.

Schnarch, D. (2009). *Passionate Marriage: Keeping Love and Intimacy Alive in Committed Relationships.* New York: W.W. Norton.

Session Seven

INDIVIDUALIZED CARE

The past can hurt. But the way I see it, you can either run from it, or learn from it.

Robert Guillaume, *The Lion King*

I once had this couple who said they wanted the basic six sessions of pre-marital counseling. Tammy and Jacob stated they had no problems really and they were quite happy. They just wanted to do pre-marital counseling because their church and family members suggested it would be a good step. Once we started discussing some of the skills in previous sessions, I began to see a different picture. Tammy often felt Jacob didn't listen to her during conflict. Tammy sometimes drank more than Jacob was comfortable with. As I continued to work with them, I uncovered more and more pieces.

There is no cookie cutter approach to working with a couple. Each person is unique and has different personal histories. As clinicians, we need to find a way to individualize the care we give so that clients can get the most out of our pre-marital counseling sessions. As in the example of Tammy and Jacob, your couples can still benefit from the basic pre-marital skills. However, you will often find your clients need more specific guidance in different areas of their lives.

In this session, clinicians should be focused on specific issues that pre-marital clients would like to address. Usually, in the assessment session, your clients will discuss specific areas that may need work. L.A. Kurdek (1994) grouped the most common areas of conflict into six categories including "power, social issues, personal flaws, distrust, intimacy, and personal distance" (Meza-de-Luna and Romero-Zepeda, 2013, p. 88). The most common additional discussions I have needed to have with my pre-marital couples in these categories involve loyalty issues with in-laws, parenting/co-parenting issues, financial differences, division of daily labor and personal time, and differences in life goals. More serious problems that you may see in pre-marital counseling include mental illnesses, substance abuse, trust issues, interpersonal violence, and infidelities. Clinicians can use this session to delve deeper into the specific issues a couple needs to address and give helpful ideas for how they can work better as a team. In some cases, clinicians may need to suggest that an individual or a couple requires longer-term care than is offered in the basic eight-session model.

This chapter is written differently than previous chapters, to go over a few of the most common issues I see in pre-marital counseling. It is meant to offer a few ideas for how clinicians can help clients address specific issues. The sections included will offer suggestions for how to discuss financial problems, chore issues, parenting/co-parenting concerns, and problems related to in-laws. In addition, I will offer resources for books and articles that may help couples to make better decisions regarding these issues. This chapter is meant to offer some suggestions for how to handle these issues. However, it is by no means a comprehensive look at these separate issues. I am relying on you, the clinician, to seek additional research and training in these areas should you need them to guide your practice.

Financial Planning

Michael and Christine are newlyweds who are fighting about their money. Michael's parents always discussed the value of paying off debts. By the time his parents retired they had paid off their home and lived a relatively low-maintenance life. Christine's parents emphasized the value of investing their money. Rather than paying off a mortgage or any loans for that matter, they often would use extra money to invest in their retirement, a property, or their business. Now, Michael and Christine have recently gotten a bunch of money from wedding gifts and are struggling to figure out what to do with it. Michael wants to use it to pay down their student loans while Christine wants to save it for retirement. They often fight about what choice to make about any extra money.

One of the most common issues a couple fights about is money. In his research on the top areas of conflict that lead to divorce, Dew (2009) found that the five highest determinants included incompatibility, emotional support, abuse, sexual problems, and financial problems (Britt and Huston, 2012). If they have no money, they fight about being broke. If they do have money, they fight about how to use their money. The fact is that most individuals have expectations and values about how money should be saved, spent, and used. If a couple is very different in their way of handling this, problems will ensue.

In pre-marital counseling, clinicians can offer some advice to help couples begin making a financial plan for their future. In fact, it would be a huge benefit for pre-marital counselors to spend some time getting trained in this area since financial planning is not commonly addressed in pre-marital counseling (Risch et al., 2003). If you have not gotten training in this area, you can refer clients to a financial planner or financial counselor if it seems like a couple could benefit from additional counseling in this area.

In this section, there are some basic financial models I will go over. These models discuss different styles that couples can use to organize their finances. It is by no means a comprehensive look at the different financial options available, but it can be useful when working with a couple in pre-marital counseling if they have asked for help in this area.

Financial Models

The first model I commonly see is where the couple has separate bank accounts for different financial needs. For example, they will have one account that is set aside solely for the monthly bills. Each partner contributes a portion of their income to the joint account to make sure bills such as the mortgage, car payments, utilities, and other bills are always paid. In addition, they will have a separate account they use for entertainment or personal expenses. This separate account can either be a joint account or each partner will have their own account they can use for personal spending. In this model, the couple is still aware of each other's finances, but they don't bug each other too much about personal accounts as long as the family bills are paid.

A second model is where the couple only has joint accounts but they create a budget they both agree to. In this budget, they will designate how much money goes toward each bill, savings, paying off debts, entertainment, and personal budgets. A couple can use a helpful resource such as Quicken or their bank's software to organize their spending. In his book *Dave Ramsey's Complete Guide to Money: The Handbook of Financial Peace University* (Ramsey, 2015), Ramsey suggests that couples take out cash and put it in specific envelopes for personal expenses, groceries, gas, date nights, etc. He suggests cash budgets because this helps couples to pay attention to the specific amounts they spend and stay within their budgets. The idea is to only spend what they can find in their envelope and to stop spending when the cash is out. In this model, a couple is likely to discuss any big purchases as a team. They plan ahead and sometimes will even meet monthly or quarterly to renegotiate the budget.

A third model is where a couple keeps their own bank accounts and divides the bills between them. One partner will take on the car and mortgage while the other partner will pay for groceries, gas, and medical bills. They divide and conquer, and discuss bills as needed when they come up. For all the models, there is no right or wrong way to handle finances so long as each partner is on the same page and bills are taken care of. It is helpful to have regular meetings about finances where couples discuss big purchases that are coming up.

Finally, if a couple appears to need more help in this area, the following resources and books are helpful to guide couples in setting up their own financial planning:

1. *Dave Ramsey's Complete Guide to Money: The Handbook of Financial Peace University* (Ramsey, 2015).
2. *Ordinary People, Extraordinary Wealth* (Edelman, 2000).
3. *Smart Couples Finish Rich* (Bach, 2002).
4. *Why didn't they Teach me This in School?* (Siegel, 2013).

Division of Labor

Jenny and Todd, a young couple with a child, came in to discuss problems with their relationship. Before they had a child, Jenny often did the cooking and cleaning in the house. They both had full-time jobs. She didn't complain much then because, while it was annoying, she reported it was at least tolerable. She didn't feel overwhelmed by the tasks and she was good at cooking and cleaning. "If I left it up to him, he would screw it up," she stated jokingly. However, after they had their baby, the tasks became very difficult. She was exhausted taking care of their new son. Jenny and Todd started to fight a lot more. "He's the one who wanted this baby, and he doesn't help," Jenny cried.

A recent article in *Time Magazine* shows that 83–84 percent of women versus 65 percent of men report spending time on household chores, childcare, or household management (Tennery, 2012). In 2010, 60 percent of women reported being the sole income for their household. It is striking to note that even when women are working just as much and even sometimes more, they still end up taking on more of the household tasks.

In pre-marital counseling, it can be very helpful to discuss the division of labor at work, at home, and regarding childcare. In the beginning of a relationship, couples are setting the expectations for that relationship. It is important to guide individuals to ask for help and to work together as a team. "When men do more housework, wives perceptions of fairness and marital satisfaction tend to rise" (Kornrich et al., 2012, p. 27). In general, those couples I work with who demonstrate a more egalitarian style of marriage tend to be happier with each other. At this stage, it can be helpful to assess how well a couple is at dividing all the household tasks in addition to their weekly workload outside of the home.

One intervention that can be used to teach couples to work better is to have them identify every role that is needed to run a successful household. The roles can include paying and maintaining bills, shopping, household management, chores, errands, childcare, outdoor maintenance, car/house repair, and employment. Once a couple has written out every role there is, then have them list the hours it takes to complete each role. From this list, encourage the couple to identify how much time each person is putting toward the different roles. After completing the task, you can then discuss either the ways they might work shift things or help each other out better.

Sometimes, couples will realize they both are contributing a great deal to the household. However, they were unaware of everything their partner did to contribute. In these cases, I encourage couples to be more appreciative of the different tasks each person does. The reality is that there are many jobs required to maintain a household and each person deserves to feel recognized for their part in helping out.

In other cases, couples may recognize deficits in how they are maintaining their household. A clinician can be especially helpful in teaching the couple different strategies for keeping up with chores and other household tasks. Remember that cleaning is a habit like any other habit. If a couple comes up a new strategy for organization and cleaning, remind them it takes several times repeating the behavior before the new strategy will become a habit.

For couples who could use more help in this area, helpful resources to point them to include:

1. *The Second Shift* (Hochschild and Machung, 2012).
2. *The Business of Love Workbook: 9 Best Practices for Improving the Bottom Line of Your Relationship* (Curtis, 2006).

Parenting/Co-parenting

Erica and Daniel had been married for about a year. Erica reported that James was too rough with the kids. James stated she was too lax with the kids. They each had kids prior to getting married. Erica has two 13-year-old twin boys. Daniel has a 13-year-old boy and a 9-year-old girl. When Daniel and Erica got married, they got along very well. At that time, they mostly spent time together as a couple but had not lived together prior to getting married. They had met each other's kids and sometimes included the kids on dates. However, this first year of marriage had really been the first time they had lived with their children in the same house.

Parenting is a very important part of a marriage for some couples. Whether a couple plans to have kids in the future or is blending their kids into a new marriage, it is important for the couple to come up with clear plans for how to address parenting issues. Kids take up a lot of time and energy and if a couple is not working together well as a team, parenting differences can result in marriages ending. In the case of Daniel and Erica, their parenting style differences were so strong, they were considering divorce at the time they sought counseling. Had they discussed these issues in pre-marital counseling, they may have been able to plan ahead for how they could join their different families.

One parenting intervention I use in pre-marital counseling involves coming up with agreed upon house rules or family rules. I encourage the couple to sit down and discuss specific rules they want for their house to run smoothly. "Rules let everyone in the family know how to behave . . . They can also help children and teenagers feel safe and secure" (Raising Children Network, 2010). These rules can be general or more specific. For example, a rule may be, "No kicking, punching, hitting, or physical violence of any kind." Rules can also be phrased in terms of what people should do instead of what not to do: "When you are angry, go to your room until you calm down."

When parents are writing the rules, I remind them that any rule they set for their kids must be a rule they will personally take responsibility for modeling. If a parent wants their kids to use quiet voices in the house, that parent also needs to use a quiet voice when inside the house. The old adage, "Do as I say, not as I do," is not an effective parenting tool. I typically will remind parents that their kids will pick up their parents' worst habits. Instead, parents need to model the behavior they would like to see in their children. In pre-marital counseling, I encourage couples to begin to shift any behaviors now that they don't want to see in their future children if that is their plan.

After parents have written a list of rules for their home, I encourage them to write a list of their personal values for why they chose those rules. One reason for doing this is to help parents clarify with kids and with each other why the rules are set. There should be a reason for why a rule is set. For example, no violence is a rule to ensure the safety of everyone in the house. Another example, use inside voices while in the house is a rule meant to help people respect those around them.

A big reason for linking values to the rules is to help parents to follow through with any consequences they set as a result of breaking the rules. For some parents, it can be difficult to discipline their children. When rules are reframed as a means to teach kids values, it makes it easier for parents to follow through with consequences and be consistent. It also helps couples to work better together when they each know why the other person is disciplining the child. Since the couple has agreed upon why those rules should be set, when they see the other parent disciplining their child, they can remind themselves that this is what they agreed upon.

Finally, parents should be guided in coming up with a plan for how they will offer consequences both positive and negative for following and breaking the rules. This is an important part of the parenting plan because it helps them come up with consequences as a team. Examples of a consequence can include a friendly reminder, a firm reminder, time out (number of minutes equal to the age), or grounding for teenagers, loss of privileges, working to repay a debt, etc. I guide parents in discussing when to administer what consequence. I also encourage parents to come up with plans for how they can communicate with each other when they are not sure what consequence to give.

This is only one example of a parenting plan that can be taught in pre-marital counseling. Parenting can be very challenging and may require more intervention than this if they are blending a family. Since I could write an entire book about this topic, instead I will offer a few resources that can help parents get started:

1. *Mom's House, Dad's House* (Ricci, 1997).
2. *How to Talk so Kids will Listen, and Listen so Kids will Talk* (Faber and Mazlish, 2012).
3. *Raising an Emotionally Intelligent Child: The Heart of Parenting* (Gottman and Declaire, 1998).

Boundaries with In-Laws and Outsiders

Russell and Meredith were having trouble when they came into pre-marital counseling. Russell was the only child of a single mother.

He and his mother have always been close. When Russell met Meredith, he thought he had found the perfect woman. However, a few months after they started dating, tensions rose between them regarding his mother. Russell always would go to his mother for advice about different things. When Meredith and Russell fought, he commonly would talk with his mother about their issues. This made Meredith feel uncomfortable and ganged up on because often she felt Russell's mother would take his side and fuel his anger toward Meredith. Meredith wanted to make sure going forward they were working together better as a couple.

Many couples struggle with how to set clear boundaries between their romantic relationship and outsiders, such as in-laws and friends. This can be a very challenging topic because individuals greatly differ on what they consider to be appropriate. In the case of Russell listed above, his family culture is more enmeshed. Enmeshment is a concept coined by Salvador Minuchin which means that family boundaries are diffuse and family members are over-concerned about meeting others' needs rather than meeting their own (Nichols and Schwartz, 2005). He is used to seeking help from his mother. Meredith may not be as close to her parents, or she may have been raised with the value that the primary couple comes first and all other relationships are secondary. Regardless of the cultural and familial values each individual brings, clinicians need to help couples find a happy middle ground to address what information can be shared and must be kept between the romantic couple. If the couple can set clear boundaries for this topic, they will be much healthier as a couple long term.

One method to address this topic is for the clinician to ask the couple to identify specific issues they would feel uncomfortable sharing with outside parties. The clinician can help by offering their own ideas that previous clients have disagreed about. Common issues that can be offered include sex, financial issues, parenting choices, fights within the romantic relationship, and holidays. While discussing the topics, the clinician can ask questions about how comfortable they would feel if their partner disclosed information about any of the above given topics. During this discussion, the clinician should ask questions such as:

1. What topics would be okay to discuss with outside parties?
2. What topics would feel like a breach of trust?
3. Does it depend on who your partner is talking to? For example, would you be more comfortable with them seeking advice from a friend versus a family member?
4. What's an example of a situation in your past where you felt there were inappropriate boundaries between your partner and the outside party?

During this conversation, the clinician should help the couple establish clear and realistic boundaries.

One thing I often discuss with couples during this topic is finding a relationship advocate. A relationship advocate is someone who listens to their problem and tries to help that person make positive decisions that will improve their relationship. A relationship advocate can be a clinician, a good friend who doesn't take sides, or a couple that has a healthy marriage. I believe that individuals and couples can often benefit from seeking help from a third party so long as both partners agree that person is a good fit.

Some helpful resources clinicians can use to understand this further include:

1. *Toxic Inlaws* (Forward, 2002).
2. *Boundaries in Marriage* (Cloud and Townsend, 2002).

Rookie Mistakes

One common mistake clinicians make when doing pre-marital counseling is to offer a generic pre-marital counseling program to all their clients. The reality is that each couple is very different and has unique needs. The purpose of this chapter is to offer guidance for how to include more specific help that is relevant to each client's needs. Not every couple will need to discuss each of the issues covered in this chapter, but as a clinician, it is important to be able to offer assistance for a variety of pre-marital needs.

Another common mistake clinicians make is not keeping informed of the latest research on different topics. A big part of a clinician's job is to keep learning and growing professionally. While we are required to get continuing education in our field, even beyond a class here and there, we need to be reading research articles and incorporating the latest most helpful treatment options in therapy. Your practice should grow and mature, not stay the same for 20 years. As new research comes out, clinicians can learn how to shift their treatment for the better.

A final mistake clinicians can make includes only offering ideas based on your personal experience with a particular topic. While personal experience can be very helpful, it is important to offer options for clients. What works for one person does not work for every person. For example, there are actually several parenting models that are commonly used. When you ask parents which programs are most helpful, you will likely get various answers, because each child is a unique individual. As a clinician, offering options helps clients feel empowered to use the skill that will work best in their own family.

Practice Ideas

1. Ask friends, family members, and clients what they do to organize their finances. Find out what tips people would give you for how to keep things civil when they talk about money.

2. Take a financial seminar in which you learn some helpful tools for managing money. If this topic interests you, there are financial family therapy courses clinicians can take to get certified in this area.

3. Read several of the latest parenting books. From those books, pick a few ideas that you can use in your own practice to guide future or current parents.

4. Examine your own methods for keeping up with household tasks. Explore how similar your methods are to friends, family members, and clients. See if you can learn some household management tips from those people you know.

Bibliography

Allers, R. and Minkoff, R. (1994). *The Lion King*. Walt Disney Pictures.

Bach, D. (2002). *Smart Couples Finish Rich*. New York: Broadway Books.

Britt, S.L. and Huston, S.J. (2012). The role of money arguments in marriage, *Journal of Family Economic Issues, 33*, 464–476.

Cloud, H. and Townsend, J. (2002). *Boundaries in Marriage*. Orange, CA: Yates and Yates.

Curtis, J. (2006). *The Business of Love Workbook: 9 Best Practices for Improving the Bottom Line of Your Relationship*. Maitland, FL: IOD.

Dew, J.P. (2009). Financial issues as predictors of divorce. Paper presented at the *Annual Conference of the National Council on Family Relations*, San Francisco.

Edelman, R. (2000). *Ordinary People, Extraordinary Wealth*. New York: Harper Business.

Faber, A. and Mazlish, E. (2012). *How to Talk so Kids will Listen, and Listen so Kids will Talk*. New York: Avon Books.

Forward, S. (2002). *Toxic Inlaws*. New York: Harper Collins.

Gottman, J. and Declaire, J. (1998). *Raising an Emotionally Intelligent Child: The Heart of Parenting*. New York: Fireside.

Hochschild, A. and Machung, A. (2012). *The Second Shift: Working Families and the Revolution at Home*. New York: Penguin.

Kornrich, S., Brines, J., and Leupp, K. (2012). Egalitarianism, housework, and sexual frequency in marriage, *American Sociological Review, 78*(1), 26–50.

Kurdek, L.A. (1994). Areas of conflict for gay, lesbian, and heterosexual couples: What couples argue about influences relationship satisfaction, *Journal of Marriage and Family, 56*(4), 923–934.

Meza-de-Luna, M.E. and Romero-Zepeda, H. (2013). Areas of conflict in the intimate couple, *Trames, 17*(67/62), *1*, 87–100.

Nichols, M.P. and Schwartz, R.C. (2005). *Family Therapy: Concepts and Methods*. New York: Allyn and Bacon.

Raising Children Network (2010). *Family Rules*, http://raisingchildren.net.au/articles/family_rules.html.

Ramsey, D. (2015). *Dave Ramsey's Complete Guide to Money: The Handbook of Financial Peace University*. Brentwood, TN: Ramsey Press, The Lampo Group.

Ricci, I. (1997). *Mom's House, Dad's House*. New York: Fireside.

Risch, G.S., Riley, L.A., and Lawler, M.G. (2003). Problematic issues in the early years of marriage: Content for premarital education, *Journal of Psychology and Theology, 31*(3), 253–269.

Siegel, C. (2013). *Why didn't They Teach me This in School?* North Charleston, SC: Simple Strategic Solutions.

Tennery, A. (2012). More women are in the workforce—So why are they still doing so many chores? *Time Magazine*, June 28, http://business.time.com/2012/06/28/more-women-are-in-the-workforce-so-why-are-we-still-doing-so-many-chores.

Session Eight

TERMINATION AND RECOMMENDATIONS

It's not the years, honey, it's the mileage.

Harrison Ford, *Indiana Jones*

During the year I was writing this book, I was pregnant. I was researching all the different parenting advice that can be found on the internet about raising a baby. One expert suggested swaddling a baby to bed on their back. Another expert warns that you should not keep your baby on their back for too long or their head will get flat. One expert suggested singing to your child while another suggests putting the baby down without any stimulation and letting the baby cry themselves to sleep. If a person were to look at marital advice, they might find a similar story online. The reality is that each couple needs to create their own unique, happy marriage story.

Basically, what works for the couple is ultimately what is most important. Each couple will be very different in terms of what works best for them. While this book emphasizes a variety of researched ideas that can help create happy marriages, it is still the couple's responsibility to find their own happy path and maintain it. It is our job as clinicians to help guide our couples in finding that healthy path.

Through continuous work on their relationship, couples can and will have healthy successful marriages. The work involved includes all of the five habits listed in this book: 1) choosing to love; 2) being empathetic; 3) fighting respectfully; 4) asking for needs and wants effectively; and 5) keeping the spark alive. No one will have the perfect marriage, because there is no such thing. However, couples can create a satisfying marriage if they are willing to put in the work.

When to Terminate

Most of your client couples will terminate at the end of their eight sessions of pre-marital counseling. Some will even end at six weeks if they don't feel they need to address any specific issues. However, there are some scenarios where it would be beneficial for the clinician to suggest further care.

Some common reasons to suggest further care include:

1. If at least one client has an untreated mental health disorder such as bipolar, depression, anxiety, etc.
2. If at least one client has an untreated substance abuse/dependence problem.
3. If the couple is fighting a lot and not reaching helpful resolutions.
4. If there are secrets being kept from each other that could harm the relationship.
5. If either partner is still reporting serious reservations about whether getting married is a good idea, that is "getting cold feet."
6. If clients request further care.

If there is any clinical reason that a clinician may find concerning, the clinician should discuss that with their clients.

Usually at about the sixth or seventh session, a clinician should know whether or not it would be a good idea to continue with treatment or to terminate treatment. At this point, the best approach to take is to bring up termination directly with your clients. I usually will state something such as, "At this point, we had planned to terminate by session 8. I wanted to make sure we were still on that path or if anything had changed regarding your plans." This gives your clients an option to either discuss adding sessions or let you know they still plan to terminate. If clients report they are finished and ready to terminate, then make your final session plans and continue with your original treatment plan.

However, if you do think that a couple needs longer term care, part of your eighth session should be a discussion of what problems you foresee in their relationship and what steps you think would be most helpful to address those issues. Since it may still end up being a termination session, regardless of your opinions, make sure you state whatever you think is important for them to hear. For example, if you clearly see a bipolar diagnosis, you should let them know what symptoms you see, what your concerns are about untreated bipolar, and what specific steps they could take to treat bipolar should they choose to do so.

Once you have discussed any foreseeable problems with your couple, it is ultimately up to them as to whether or not they will continue with treatment or end things. Even if a couple chooses to terminate when you think they should not, remind them you are always available should they need you in the future. This way, the door is open for future treatment. Sometimes in these cases, I will give a follow up call or email to check in about 6 months after termination. This way you can have peace of mind regarding their best possible care.

Helping Couples Set Long-term Life Goals

One common intervention a clinician can use in this final session is to help their couple set life goals. In this intervention, you give each partner a notebook and have them make three columns. One column is for 1-year goals. One column is for 3-year goals. One column is for 5-year goals. Then, you set up the intervention by asking them to think about what goals they have for their future. Include topics such as financial goals, becoming parents, professional goals, life goals, leisure and fun goals, and anything the couple can think about. Then, instruct the couple to write down as many goals they can think of personally to add to each list. Give them about 10 minutes to write their individual goals. Then, have them compare their lists and talk about similarities or differences.

This goal list is a great way to help the couple begin planning their future together. Clinicians can guide couples to ask more in-depth questions about goals such as how they will plan for their future trips, or how they will compromise if one person is asked to move for their job. This intervention can be helpful in getting couples thinking about their choices and how these choices will affect their partners. This intervention can be a fun way to terminate treatment because it gets couples feeling hopeful about their future.

Developing Strategies for Hard Times

Another potential thing you can do in the termination session is to give couples a clear picture of what married life truly looks like. In every relationship, there are inevitably good times and bad times. This session is your final chance to give your clients words of wisdom that can be helpful to them as they start their marriage.

Long ago, I had my own pre-marital counseling sessions before my husband and I got married. I remember one statement our counselor said that has stayed with me throughout the years: "You will have good days and bad days; good weeks and bad weeks; good years and bad years." I had heard about good days and bad ones but I had never thought about full years being difficult in marriage. I appreciated this advice later in my marriage when my husband and I were going through a tough year. Your clients will remember some of your words of wisdom as well. So take this session as an opportunity to offer guidance.

Clinicians can offer guidance by explaining some of the challenges a couple may go through that are long-term challenges. These could include infertility, the unexpected death of a loved one, divorce of family members, a disability or long-term physical illness, a depression or breakdown, etc. After discussing some of these life challenges, the clinician can talk to their couple about creating a plan to seek help.

One of the biggest struggles couples have during these times is not knowing who to turn to for support and struggling to support each other effectively. There are different reasons for this challenge. For one, when an issue is short and easily resolvable, usually a couple will figure out a solution and move on. In these circumstances, there is no clear or easy solution. The problem is long term and it gets harder to work through problems and be empathetic when a problem seems to have no end. For example, in the case of infertility, couples will go through several different options on their path to trying to conceive. With each failure, it gets harder for them to struggle on. The couple may begin to argue more about little things because the big issue—having a baby—just won't resolve itself. With each failure, the couple must grieve and come to accept the next step in the fertility process.

A second struggle couples face when dealing with long-term issues is who to turn to outside of the relationship. No couple should be forced to go through life's challenges alone. It helps to get support from family, friends, and community, specifically to be able to discuss challenges with others who have been there. This can be extremely helpful when these outside parties can commiserate or offer advice for how they personally got through hard times. Seeking help outside the marriage can be a struggle because culturally it appears people are becoming more private about their problems with outside parties. I have recognized in the couples I work with that when they go through these big life struggles, they often have not shared anything with family or friends. When asked why, they state they don't know who to go to, or they don't want to burden others.

Instead I often find people seeking support online from others who are going through similar issues because this can be an anonymous forum. This can still be a helpful means for an individual to seek support, but it is no substitute for having a person in your life in addition to a spouse who is advocating for the marriage and the health of the individuals.

In session, clinicians can guide couples to discuss who they feel confident going to for support outside of the marriage. Clients can identify family, friends, and even counselors depending on the severity of the situation. Clinicians can suggest couples come up with a plan for when and how they decide they need professional help.

Toward the end of pre-marital counseling, clinicians should focus on offering hope for the future. Above all, clients want hope that their relationship is going to succeed. Clinicians can offer some hope by stating many of the strengths they have recognized in their clients. Usually, I will discuss challenges they have overcome well in sessions. I also discuss ways that their personalities complement each other. Basically, it helps to end using a strengths-based approach while also reminding the couple that they are always free to come back should they need help in the future. Some clinicians may decide to write a positive termination letter outlining all the strengths they see in the couple relationship. This can be a very positive thing to send a couple after their pre-marital counseling terminated.

Wrapping Up

In this book, we have discussed the five principles for a successful marriage. Those principles include fighting respectfully, being empathetic, choosing to love, maintaining the spark, and asking for needs and wants effectively. Clinicians have learned different ways to structure each session for pre-marital counseling, and specific interventions that can be used to help couples learn the five principles so they can work on keeping a healthy vital marriage. Finally, clinicians have also learned ways to tailor their treatment plan to each individual couple.

Through writing this book, researching each topic in depth, and working with many couples in therapy, I have learned a few things I didn't expect to learn. First, couples often surprise me, and second, I can learn something new from each client I work with.

Couples are surprising in their resilience. There have been many times when I thought a couple was ready to throw in the towel, only to see them come back full force ready to improve the situation. Just because I have worked with many couples does not mean I have every answer, nor does it mean I will be able to solve all their problems. While this book shows some common traits these couples use to improve their situation, there have been other couples who used very out of the ordinary means to improve as well. For example, I have had couples who completely divorced each other only to rekindle after several months. I have seen other couples fight unfairly and for very long periods only to come back feeling as though they finally cleared the air and were able to discuss their issues again. While these tools are meant to help guide couples to improve their situation, sometimes, couples need to use their own resources regardless of a clinician's opinion about what should be considered fair.

The second surprising thing is how much I can learn from each client I work with. Some of the skills listed in this book came directly from the couples I have helped in therapy. By listening to their issues and giving them a space to figure things out, couples teach me a variety of new ways to resolve issues and get along better as a team. I encourage every clinician reading this book to keep a strong curiosity and an ability to learn because you never know what your clients can teach you. For example, I had a couple in which one person was more introverted and the other more extroverted. They had learned that it is more helpful for them to set an agenda for future discussions a day or two in advance so that the introverted person had some time to formulate their opinion about the situation. This small shift in their discussions helped them create helpful resolutions that worked for both of them.

The most helpful advice I can give to all clinicians in this field is to be flexible in your approach. Use this book as a tool for helping couples create pro-social skills. But in the end, trust your clients' judgment for their own lives. They are the ones responsible for the consequences of their choices. We are merely guides in that path.

Bibliography

Spielberg, S. (1981). *Indiana Jones*. Lucasfilm.

INDEX